THE
REFERENCE
SHELF

# REPRESENTATIVE

# AMERICAN SPEECHES,

# 1994–1995

Edited by OWEN PETERSON
Professor, Department of Speech Communication
Louisiana State University

THE REFERENCE SHELF

Volume 67 Number 6

THE H. W. WILSON COMPANY

New York   Dublin   1995

# THE REFERENCE SHELF

The books in this series contain reprints of articles, excerpts from books, addresses on current issues, and studies of social trends in the United States and other countries. There are six numbers to a volume, all of which are usually published in a single calendar year. Numbers one through five devote themselves to a single subject, give background information and discussion from various points of view, concluding with a comprehensive bibliography that contains books, pamphlets and abstracts of additional articles on the subject. The final number is a collection of recent speeches. This number also contains a subject index to the entire Reference Shelf volume. Books in the series may be purchased individually or on subscription.

**Library of Congress Cataloging-in-Publication Data**

Representative American speeches. 1937/38–
    New York, H. W. Wilson Co.
        v. 21 cm.—(The Reference shelf)
    Annual.
    Indexes:
        Author index: 1937/38–1959/60, with 1959/60;
        1960/61–1969/70, with 1969/70; 1970/71–1979/80,
        with 1979/80; 1980/81–1989/90, with 1990.
    Editors: 1937/38–1958/59, A. C. Baird.—1959/60—1969/70, L.
    Thonssen.—1970/71–1979/80, W. W. Braden.—1980/81— O.
    Peterson.
    ISSN 0197-6923 Representative American speeches.
    ISBN 8242-0885-4
    1. Speeches, addresses, etc., American.   2. Speeches, addresses, etc.
    I. Baird, Albert Craig, 1883–1979 ed. II. Thonssen,
    Lester, 1904– ed. III. Braden, Waldo Warder, 1911–1991 ed.
    IV. Peterson, Owen, 1924– ed. V. Series.
PS668.B3                       815.5082                  38-27962
                                                        MARC-S

Library of Congress [8503r85]rev4

Printed in the United States of America

# CONTENTS

PREFACE .......................................... 7

## I. POLITICAL CHOICES AND CHANGE

William J. Clinton. State of the Union Address ......... 9
Newton L. Gingrich. A Contract With America ......... 30
Edward M. Kennedy. Commitment to Values .......... 41
Mario M. Cuomo. A Farewell to Public Office .......... 50
Henry J. Hyde. Congressional Term Limits ............ 65

## II. VIOLENCE AND TERRORISM

F. Forrester Church IV. Fear and Terror ............... 71
D. Stanley Eitzen. Violent Crime: Myths, Facts,
    and Solutions ................................... 78

## III. IMPACT OF THE MASS MEDIA

Andrew A. Rooney. Television News Reporting ......... 88
Bruce E. Gronbeck. Electric Rhetoric: The Transformation
    of American Political Talk ........................ 95

## IV. THE AFRICAN AMERICAN EXPERIENCE

William B. Gould IV. Lincoln, Labor, and the Black Military:
    The Legacy Provided ............................ 111
Vernon E. Jordan, Jr. The Struggle Is Not Over ........ 120

V. FOREIGN POLICY DIRECTIONS

George F. Kennan. Defining American Foreign Policy .... 128
James R. Schlesinger. American Leadership, Isolationism,
    and Unilateralism ................................. 132


VI. REAFFIRMING VALUES

Jane Alexander. The Arts and Education .............. 143
Jack J. Valenti. William Faulkner's Old Verities:
    It's Planting Time in America ...................... 149


VII. IN REMEMBRANCE

F. Forrester Church IV. An American Creed ........... 156
Elie Wiesel. Close Your Eyes, and Listen
    to the Silent Screams ............................. 163


APPENDIX: BIOGRAPHICAL NOTES ...................... 167

CUMULATIVE SPEAKER INDEX: 1990–1995 .............. 173

CUMULATIVE INDEX TO REFERENCE SHELF VOLUME 67 ..... 177

# PREFACE

This collection of *Representative American Speeches* is the fourteenth volume I have prepared. My association with the series goes back to the 1940s when I first encountered it as an undergraduate student in the classes of A. Craig Baird at the University of Iowa. Professor Baird started the series in 1937 to fill what he perceived as a need for contemporary speech models for students. From the beginning, he insisted that the speeches were not necessarily the best, but were *representative*. Baird edited the series for 22 years. Since then, all three succeeding editors—Lester Thonssen (1959–1970), Waldo W. Braden (1970–1980), and myself (1980 to present)—have been former students of Dr. Baird at Iowa. I think all of us shared his philosophy and tried to maintain his standards in the selection of speeches. In 1992, the Speech Communication Association recognized the series when it presented a special Winans-Wichelns award for distinguished scholarship to the four editors.

I often am asked two questions: where I obtain speeches and how many I consider each year. As for the first question, newspapers, magazines, and the broadcast media seldom provide complete texts of speeches, but they often report an event and summarize the speaker's remarks. With this information, it is a simple matter for the editor to write the speaker or the event's sponsor requesting the complete text. In my experience, they are almost always responsive.

How many speeches do I consider each year? In the beginning, I didn't keep track of the figure, but I was asked the question so often that I decided to make a count. I know now that I usually read (often skim) between 500 and 600 speeches a year.

What kinds of speeches are chosen? Over the past fourteen years the types of addresses reprinted have included lectures, sermons, eulogies, welcomes, farewells, inaugurals, as well as speeches at commencement exercises, conventions, conferences, commemorative occasions, and award presentations. The topics have ranged across the arts, business, crime, economics, education, foreign affairs, labor, law, the media, medicine, philosophy, politics, race, religion, science, and sports, among many others.

In preparing the volume, I have been greatly assisted by many people. I am indebted to Bruce R. Carrick, Editor of General

Publications at The H. W. Wilson Company. Throughout my editorship, he has always been cooperative, helpful, encouraging, and tolerant of my delays and mistakes. The Department of Speech Communication at Louisiana State University has been supportive at all times. In my prefaces to earlier volumes, I have acknowledged the valuable contributions of research assistants and undergraduate student workers. In addition, department colleagues and former students interested in American public address have been very helpful in calling to my attention significant speeches I might otherwise have missed.

For this volume, I owe special thanks to my research assistant Claire Hopson, who tracked down much of the background information on the audiences, occasions, and speeches. I also appreciate the valuable contribution of Alison Rodriguez, who for the second year worked on the preparation of the manuscript. As usual, Ginger Conrad and Lisa Landry were cooperative and helpful.

OWEN PETERSON

Baton Rouge, Louisiana
September 30, 1995

# POLITICAL CHOICES AND CHANGE

## STATE OF THE UNION ADDRESS[1]
### WILLIAM J. CLINTON[2]

When President Bill Clinton delivered the traditional annual State of the Union speech to Congress and the American people on January 24, 1995, he faced a situation quite different from the one in which he had delivered his two previous State of the Union addresses. Elected in 1992 after twelve years of Republican presidents with Democratic majorities in both the House and Senate, President Clinton after the 1994 elections was suddenly confronted with the problem of providing leadership in a government with Republican majorities in both Houses of Congress.

President Clinton's State of the Union message, covered most of the topics and themes of his administration. At one hour and twenty-one minutes, Clinton's speech was the longest State of the Union address in American history. The explanation seems to have been that presidential aides and Mrs. Clinton felt that the final forty-minute draft of the speech did not sound like the President and urged him to recast it in his own words. Following this advice, the President dictated extensive last-minute revisions, tinkering with the speech until he set off for the Capitol at 8:30 p.m. [Douglas Jehl, *New York Times*, January 26, 1995, p.A9]

In spite of the length of the speech, television surveys showed that forty-six percent of all viewers on the four major networks watched the President's address.

As is usual, a spokesperson from the opposition party was given television time to respond to the presidential address. The speaker chosen by the Republicans was Governor Christine Todd Whitman of New Jersey.

*President Clinton's speech:* Mr. President, Mr. Speaker, members of the 104th Congress, my fellow Americans, again we are here in the sanctuary of democracy. And once again, our democracy has spoken.

[1]Delivered in the United States House of Representatives at 9:00 p.m. on January 24, 1995.

[2]For biographical note, see Appendix.

So let me begin by congratulating all of you here in the 104th Congress, and congratulating you, Mr. Speaker.

If we agree on nothing else tonight, we must agree that the American people certainly voted for change in 1992 and in 1994.

And as I look out at you, I know how some of you must have felt in 1992.

I must say that in both years we didn't hear America singing, we heard America shouting. And now all of us, Republicans and Democrats alike, must say: We hear you. We will work together to earn the jobs you have given us. For we are the keepers of the sacred trust and we must be faithful to it in this new and very demanding era.

Over 200 years ago, our founders changed the entire course of human history by joining together to create a new country based on a single, powerful idea. We hold these truths to be self-evident, that all men are created equal, endowed by their creator with certain inalienable rights. Among these are life, liberty and the pursuit of happiness.

It has fallen to every generation since then to preserve that idea—the American idea—and to deepen and expand its meaning in new and different times. To Lincoln and to his Congress, to preserve the Union and to end slavery. To Theodore Roosevelt and Woodrow Wilson, to restrain the abuses and excesses of the Industrial Revolution and to assert our leadership in the world. To Franklin Roosevelt, to fight the failure and pain of the Great Depression and to win our country's great struggle against fascism.

And to all our Presidents since, to fight the cold war. Especially, I recall two who struggled to fight that cold war in partnership with Congresses where the majority was of a different party. To Harry Truman, who summoned us to unparalleled prosperity at home and who built the architecture of the cold war. And to Ronald Reagan, whom we wish well tonight, and who exorted us to carry on until the twilight struggle against Communism was won.

In another time of change and challenge, I had the honor to be the first President to be elected in the post-cold-war era, an era marked by the global economy, the information revolution, unparalleled change in opportunity and in security for the American people.

I came to this hallowed chamber two years ago on a mission: To restore the American dream for all our people and to make sure that we move into the 21st century still the strongest force for freedom and democracy in the entire world.

I was determined then to tackle the tough problems too long ignored. In this effort I am frank to say that I have made my mistakes. And I have learned again the importance of humility in all human endeavor.

But I am also proud to say tonight that our country is stronger than it was two years ago.

Record numbers, record numbers of Americans are succeeding in the new global economy. We are at peace, and we are a force for peace and freedom throughout the world. We have almost six million new jobs since I became President, and we have the lowest combined rate of unemployment and inflation in 25 years.

Our businesses are more productive and here we have worked to bring the deficit down, to expand trade, to put more police on our streets, to give our citizens more of the tools they need to get an education and to rebuild their own communities. But the rising tide is not lifting all the boats.

While our nation is enjoying peace and prosperity, too many of our people are still working harder and harder for less and less. While our businesses are restructuring and growing more productive and competitive, too many of our people still can't be sure of having a job next year or even next month. And far more than our material riches are threatened, things far more precious to us: our children, our families, our values.

Our civil life is suffering in America today. Citizens are working together less and shouting at each other more. The common bonds of community which have been the great strength of our country from its very beginning are badly frayed.

What are we to do about it?

More than 60 years ago at the dawn of another new era, President Roosevelt told our nation new conditions impose new requirements on government and those who conduct government. And from that simple proposition he shaped the New Deal, which helped to restore our nation to prosperity and defined the relationship between our people and their government for half a century.

That approach worked in its time but today we face a very different time and very different conditions. We are moving from an industrial age built on gears and sweat to an information age demanding skills and learning and flexibility.

Our government, once a champion of national purpose, is

now seen by many as simply a captive of narrow interests putting more burdens on our citizens rather than equipping them to get ahead. The values that used to hold us all together seem to be coming apart.

So tonight we must forge a new social compact to meet the challenges of this time. As we enter a new era, we need a new set of understandings not just with government but, even more important, with one another as Americans.

That's what I want to talk with you about tonight. I call it the New Covenant but it's grounded in a very, very old idea that all Americans have not just a right but a solemn responsibility to rise as far as their God-given talents and determination can take them. And to give something back to their communities and their country in return.

Opportunity and responsibility—they go hand in hand; we can't have one without the other, and our national community can't hold together without both.

Our New Covenant is a new set of understandings for how we can equip our people to meet the challenges of the new economy, how we can change the way our government works to fit a different time and, above all, how we can repair the damaged bonds in our society and come together behind our common purpose. We must have dramatic change in our economy, our government and ourselves.

My fellow Americans, without regard to party, let us rise to the occasion. Let us put aside partisanship and pettiness and pride. As we embark on this course, let us put our country first, remembering that regardless of party label we are all Americans. And let the final test of everything we do be a simple one: Is it good for the American people?

Let me begin by saying that we cannot ask Americans to be better citizens if we are not better servants. You made a good start by passing that law which applies to Congress all the laws you put on the private sector—and I was proud to sign it yesterday.

But we have a lot more to do before people really trust the way things work around here. Three times as many lobbyists are in the streets and corridors of Washington as were here 20 years ago. The American people look at their capital and they see a city where the well-connected and the well-protected can work the system, but the interests of ordinary citizens are often left out.

As the new Congress opened its doors, lobbyists were still doing business as usual—the gifts, the trips—all the things that people are concerned about haven't stopped.

Twice this month you missed opportunities to stop these practices. I know there were other considerations in those votes, but I want to use something that I've heard my Republican friends say from time to time: There doesn't have to be a law for everything.

So tonight I ask you to just stop taking the lobbyists' perks, just stop.

We don't have to wait for legislation to pass to send a strong signal to the American people that things are really changing. But I also hope you will send me the strongest possible lobby reform bill, and I'll sign that, too. We should require lobbyists to tell the people for whom they work, what they're spending, what they want. We should also curb the role of big money in elections by capping the cost of campaigns and limiting the influence of PAC's.

And as I have said for three years, we should work to open the air waves so that they can be an instrument of democracy, not a weapon of destruction, by giving free TV time to candidates for public office.

When the last Congress killed political reform last year, it was reported in the press that the lobbyists actually stood in the halls of this sacred building and cheered. This year, let's give the folks at home something to cheer about.

More important, I think we all agree that we have to change the way the government works. Let's make it smaller, less costly and smarter. Leaner not meaner.

I just told the Speaker the equal time doctrine's alive and well.

The New Covenant approach to governing is as different from the old bureaucratic way as the computer is from the manual typewriter. The old way of governing around here protected organized interests; we should look out for the interests of ordinary people. The old way divided us by interests, constituency or class; the New Covenant way should unite us behind a common vision of what's best for our country.

The old way dispensed services through large, top-down, inflexible bureaucracies. The New Covenant way should shift these resources and decision making from bureaucrats to citizens, injecting choice and competition and individual responsibility into national policy.

The old way of governing around here actually seemed to reward failure. The New Covenant way should have built-in incentives to reward success.

The old way was centralized here in Washington. The New Covenant way must take hold in the communities all across America, and we should help them to do that.

Our job here is to expand opportunity, not bureaucracy, to empower people to make the most of their own lives and to enhance our security here at home and abroad.

We must not ask government to do what we should do for ourselves. We should rely on government as a partner to help us to do more for ourselves and for each other.

I hope very much that as we debate these specific and exciting matters, we can go beyond the sterile discussion between the illusion that there is somehow a program for every problem, on the one hand, and the other illusion that the government is the source of every problem that we have.

Our job is to get rid of yesterday's government so that our own people can meet today's and tomorrow's needs.

And we ought to do it together.

You know, for years before I became President, I heard others say they would cut government and how bad it was. But not much happened.

We actually did it. We cut over a quarter of a trillion dollars in spending, more than 300 domestic programs, more than 100,000 positions from the federal bureaucracy in the last two years alone.

Based on decisions already made, we will have cut a total of more than a quarter of a million positions from the federal government, making it the smallest it has been since John Kennedy was President, by the time I come here again next year.

Under the leadership of Vice President Gore, our initiatives have already saved taxpayers $63 billion. The age of the $500 hammer and the ashtray you can break on David Letterman is gone. Deadwood programs like mohair subsidies are gone. We've streamlined the Agriculture Department by reducing it by more than 1,200 offices. We've slashed the small-business loan form from an inch thick to a single page. We've thrown away the government's 10,000-page personnel manual.

And the government is working better in important ways. FEMA, the Federal Emergency Management Agency, has gone from being a disaster to helping people in disaster.

You can ask the farmers in the Middle West who fought the flood there or the people in California who've dealt with floods and earthquakes and fires and they'll tell you that.

Government workers, working hand-in-hand with private business, rebuilt Southern California's fractured freeways in record time and under budget.

And because the federal government moved fast, all but one

of the 5,600 schools damaged in the earthquake are back in business.

Now, there are a lot of other things that I could talk about. I want to just mention one because it'll be discussed here in the next few weeks.

University administrators all over the country have told me that they are saving weeks and weeks of bureaucratic time now because of our direct college loan program, which makes college loans cheaper and more affordable with better repayment terms for students, costs the government less and cuts out paperwork and bureaucracy for the government and for the universities.

We shouldn't cap that program, we should give every college in America the opportunity to be a part of it.

Previous government programs gather dust; the reinventing government report is getting results. And we're not through—there's going to be a second round of reinventing government.

We propose to cut $130 billion in spending by shrinking departments, extending our freeze on domestic spending, cutting 60 public housing programs down to 3, getting rid of over a hundred programs we do not need like the Interstate Commerce Commission and the Helium Reserve Program.

And we're working on getting rid of unnecessary regulations and making them more sensible. The programs and regulations that have outlived their usefulness should go. We have to cut yesterday's government to help solve tomorrow's problems.

And we need to get government closer to the people it's meant to serve. We need to help move programs down to the point where states and communities and private citizens in the private sector can do a better job. If they can do it, we ought to let them do it. We should get out of the way and let them do what they can do better.

Taking power away from federal bureaucracies and giving it back to communities and individuals is something everyone should be able to be for. It's time for Congress to stop passing onto the states the cost of decisions we make here in Washington.

I know there are still serious differences over the details of the unfunded mandates legislation but I want to work with you to make sure we pass a reasonable bill which will protect the national interest and give justified relief where we need to give it.

For years, Congress concealed in the budget scores of pet spending projects. Last year was no different. There was a million dollars to study stress in plants and $12 million for a tick removal program that didn't work. It's hard to remove ticks; those of us who've had them know.

But I'll tell you something. If you'll give me the line-item veto, I'll remove some of that unnecessary spending.

But, I think we should all remember, and almost all of us would agree, that government still has important responsibilities.

Our young people—we should think of this when we cut— our young people hold our future in their hands. We still owe a debt to our veterans. And our senior citizens have made us what we are.

Now, my budget cuts a lot. But it protects education, veterans, Social Security and Medicare, and I hope you will do the same thing. You should, and I hope you will.

And when we give more flexibility to the states, let us remember that there are certain fundamental national needs that should be addressed in every state, north and south, east and west.

Immunization against childhood disease, school lunches in all our schools, Head Start, medical care and nutrition for pregnant women and infants—all these things are in the national interest.

I applaud your desire to get rid of costly and unnecessary regulations, but when we deregulate let's remember what national action in the national interest has given us: safer food for our families, safer toys for our children, safer nursing homes for our parents, safer cars and highways and safer workplaces, cleaner air and cleaner water. Do we need common sense and fairness in our regulations? You bet we do. But we can have common sense and still provide for safe drinking water. We can have fairness and still clean up toxic dumps and we ought to do it.

Should we cut the deficit more? Well of course we should. Of course we should. But we can bring it down in a way that still protects our economic recovery and does not unduly punish people who should not be punished, but instead should be helped.

I know many of you in this chamber support the balanced-budget amendment. I certainly want to balance the budget. Our Administration has done more to bring the budget down and to save money than any in a very, very long time.

If you believe passing this amendment is the right thing to do, then you have to be straight with the American people. They have a right to know what you're going to cut, what taxes you're going to raise, how it's going to affect them.

And we should be doing things in the open around here. For example, everybody ought to know if this proposal is going to endanger Social Security. I would oppose that, and I think most Americans would.

Nothing is done more to undermine our sense of common responsibility than our failed welfare system. This is one of the problems we have to face here in Washington in our New Covenant. It rewards welfare over work, it undermines family values, it lets millions of parents get away without paying their child support, it keeps a minority—but a significant minority—of the people on welfare trapped on it for a very long time.

I worked on this problem for a long time—nearly 15 years now. As a Governor I had the honor of working with the Reagan administration to write the last welfare reform bill back in 1988.

In the last two years we made a good start in continuing the work of welfare reform. Our administration gave two dozen states the right to slash through federal rules and regulations to reform their own welfare systems and to try to promote work and responsibility over welfare and dependency.

Last year, I introduced the most sweeping welfare reform plan ever presented by an administration. We have to make welfare what it was meant to be—a second chance, not a way of life.

We have to help those on welfare move to work as quickly as possible, to provide child care and teach them skills, if that's what they need, for up to two years. But after that, there ought to be a simple, hard rule. Anyone who can work must go to work.

If a parent isn't paying child support, they should be forced to pay.

We should suspend driver's licenses, track them across state lines, make them work off what they owe. That is what we should do. Governments do not raise children, people do. And the parents must take responsibility for the children they bring into this world.

I want to work with you, with all of you, to pass welfare reform. But our goal must be to liberate people and lift them from dependence to independence, from welfare to work, from mere childbearing to responsible parenting. Our goal should not be to punish them because they happen to be poor.

We should—we should require work and mutual responsibility. But we shouldn't cut people off just because they're poor, they're young or even because they're unmarried. We should promote responsibility by requiring young mothers to live at home with their parents or in other supervised settings, by requiring them to finish school. But we shouldn't put them and their children out on the street.

And I know all the arguments pro and con and I have read

and thought about this for a long time: I still don't think we can, in good conscience, punish poor children for the mistakes of their parents.

My fellow Americans, every single survey shows that all the American people care about this, without regard to party or race or religion. So let this be the year we end welfare as we know it.

But also let this be the year that we are all able to stop using this issue to divide America.

No one is more eager to end welfare.

I may be the only President who's actually had the opportunity to sit in the welfare office, who's actually spent hours and hours talking to people on welfare, and I am telling you the people who are trapped on it know it doesn't work. They also want to get off.

So we can promote, together, education and work and good parenting. I have no problem with punishing bad behavior or the refusal to be a worker or a student or a responsible parent. I just don't want to punish poverty and past mistakes. All of us have made our mistakes and none of us can change our yesterdays, but every one of us can change our tomorrows.

And America's best example of that may be Lynn Woolsey, who worked her way off welfare to become a congresswoman from the state of California.

I know the members of this Congress are concerned about crime, as are all the citizens of our country. But I remind you that last year we passed a very tough crime bill—longer sentences, three strikes and you're out, almost 60 new capital punishment offenses, more prisons, more prevention, 100,000 more police— and we paid for it all by reducing the size of the federal bureaucracy and giving the money back to local communities to lower the crime rate.

There may be other things we can do to be tougher on crime, to be smarter with crime, to help to lower that rate first.

Well if there are, let's talk about them and let's do them. But let's not go back on the things that we did last year that we know work—that we know work because the local law-enforcement officers tell us that we did the right thing. Because local community leaders, who've worked for years and years to lower the crime rate, tell us that they work.

Let's look at the experience of our cities and our rural areas where the crime rate has gone down and ask the people who did it how they did it and if what we did last year supports the decline in the crime rate, and I am convinced that it does, let us not go back on it, let's stick with it, implement it—we've got four more hard years of work to do that.

I don't want to destroy the good atmosphere in the room or in the country tonight, but I have to mention one issue that divided this body greatly last year. The last Congress also passed the Brady Bill and in the crime bill the ban on 19 assault weapons.

I don't think it's a secret to anybody in this room that several members of the last Congress who voted for that aren't here tonight because they voted for it. And I know, therefore, that some of you that are here because they voted for it are under enormous pressure to repeal it. I just have to tell you how I feel about it.

The members who voted for that bill and I would never do anything to infringe on the right to keep and bear arms to hunt and to engage in other appropriate sporting activities. I've done it since I was a boy, and I'm going to keep right on doing it until I can't do it anymore.

But a lot of people laid down their seats in Congress so that police officers and kids wouldn't have to lay down their lives under a hail of assault-weapon attacks, and I will not let that be repealed. I will not let it be repealed.

I'd like to talk about a couple of other issues we have to deal with. I want us to cut more spending, but I hope we won't cut government programs that help to prepare us for the new economy, promote responsibility and are organized from the grass roots up, not by federal bureaucracy.

The very best example of this is the National Service Corps—Americorps. It passed with strong bipartisan support and now there are 20,000 Americans—more than ever served in one year in the Peace Corps—working all over this country, helping person to person in local grass-roots volunteer groups, solving problems and in the process earning some money for their education.

This is citizenship at its best. It's good for the Americorps members, but it's good for the rest of us, too. It's the essence of the New Covenant and we shouldn't stop it.

All Americans, not only in the states most heavily affected, but in every place in this country are rightly disturbed by the large numbers of illegal aliens entering our country.

The jobs they hold might otherwise be held by citizens or legal immigrants. The public services they use impose burdens on our taxpayers. That's why our administration has moved aggressively to secure our borders more, by hiring a record number of new border guards, by deporting twice as many criminal aliens as ever before, by cracking down on illegal hiring, by barring welfare benefits to illegal aliens.

In the budget I will present to you, we will try to do more to speed the deportation of illegal aliens who are arrested for crimes, to better identify illegal aliens in the workplace as recommended by the commission headed by former Congresswoman Barbara Jordan.

We are a nation of immigrants, but we are also a nation of laws. It is wrong and ultimately self-defeating for a nation of immigrants to permit the kind of abuse of our immigration laws we have seen in recent years, and we must do more to stop it.

The most important job of our government in this new era is to empower the American people to succeed in the global economy. America has always been a land of opportunity, a land where, if you work hard, you can get ahead. We've become a great middle-class country; middle-class values sustain us. We must expand that middle class and shrink the underclass even as we do everything we can to support the millions of Americans who are already successful in the new economy.

America is once again the world's strongest economic power: almost six million new jobs in the last two years, exports booming, inflation down, high-wage jobs are coming back. A record number of American entrepreneurs are living the American dream.

If we want to stay that way, those who work and lift our nation must have more of its benefits.

Today, too many of those people are being left out. They're working harder for less. They have less security, less income, less certainty that they can even afford a vacation, much less college for their kids or retirement for themselves.

We cannot let this continue. If we don't act, our economy will probably keep doing what it's been doing since about 1978, when the income growth began to go to those at the very top of our economic scale. And the people in the vast middle got very little growth and people who worked like crazy but were on the bottom then, fell even further and further behind in the years afterward, no matter how hard they worked.

We've got to have a government that can be a real partner in making this new economy work for all of our people, a government that helps each and every one of us to get an education and to have the opportunity to renew our skills.

That's why we worked so hard to increase educational opportunities in the last two years from Head Start to public schools to apprenticeships for young people who don't go to college, to making college loans more available and more affordable.

That's the first thing we have to do: We've got to do something to empower people to improve their skills.

Second thing we ought to do is to help people raise their incomes immediately by lowering their taxes.

We took the first step in 1993 with a working family tax cut for 15 million families with incomes under $27,000, a tax cut that this year will average about $1,000 a family.

And we also gave tax reductions to most small and new businesses. Before we could do more than that, we first had to bring down the deficit we inherited and we had to get economic growth up. Now we've done both, and now we can cut taxes in a more comprehensive way.

But tax cuts should reinforce and promote our first obligation: to empower our citizens through education and training to make the most of their own lives. The spotlight should shine on those who make the right choices for themselves, their families and their communities.

I have proposed a middle-class bill of rights, which should properly be called the bill of rights and responsibilities, because its provisions only benefit those who are working to educate and raise their children and to educate themselves. It will, therefore, give needed tax relief and raise incomes, in both the short run and the long run, in a way that benefits all of us.

There are four provisions:

First, a tax deduction for all education and training after high school. If you think about it, we permit business to deduct their investment, we permit individuals to deduct interest on their home mortgages, but today an education is even more important to the economic wellbeing of our whole country than even those things are. We should do everything we can to encourage it, and I hope you will support it.

Second, we ought to cut taxes $500 for families with children under 13.

Third, we ought to foster more savings and personal responsibility by permitting people to establish an individual retirement account and withdraw from it tax free for the cost of education, health care, first-time home buying or the care of a parent.

And fourth, we should pass a G.I. Bill for America's workers.

We propose to collapse nearly 70 federal programs and not give the money to the states but give the money directly to the American people, offer vouchers to them so that they—if they're laid off or if they're working for a very low wage—can get a voucher worth $2,600 a year for up to two years to go to their local community colleges or wherever else they want to get the skills they need to improve their lives. Let's empower people in this way. Move it from the government directly to the workers of America.

Now, any one of us can call for a tax cut, but I won't accept one that explodes the deficit or puts our recovery at risk. We ought to pay for our tax cuts fully and honestly. Just two years ago it was an open question whether we would find the strength to cut the deficit.

Thanks to the courage of the people who were here then, many of whom didn't return, we did cut the deficit. We began to do what others said would not be done: We cut the deficit by over $600 billion, about $10,000 for every family in this country. It's coming down three years in a row for the first time since Mr. Truman was President and I don't think anybody in America wants us to let it explode again.

In the budget I will send you, the middle-class bill of rights is fully paid for by budget cuts in bureaucracy, cuts in programs, cuts in special interest subsidies. And the spending cuts will more than double the tax cuts. My budget pays for the middle-class bill of rights without any cuts in Medicare, and I will oppose any attempts to pay for tax cuts with Medicare cuts. That's not the right thing to do.

I know that a lot of you have your own ideas about tax relief. And some of them, I find quite interesting. I really want to work with all of you.

My tests for our proposals will be: Will it create jobs and raise incomes? Will it strengthen our families and support our children? Is it paid for? Will it build the middle class and shrink the underclass?

If it does, I'll support it. But if it doesn't, I won't.

The goal of building the middle class and shrinking the underclass is also why I believe that you should raise the minimum wage.

It rewards work—two and a half million Americans, often women with children, are working out there today for four-and-a-quarter an hour. In terms of real buying power, by next year, that minimum wage will be at a 40-year low. That's not my idea of how the new economy ought to work.

Now I studied the arguments and the evidence for and against a minimum-wage increase. I believe the weight of the evidence is that a modest increase does not cost jobs and may even lure people back into the job market. But the most important thing is you can't make a living on $4.25 an hour. Now—especially if you have children, even with the working families tax cut we passed last year.

In the past, the minimum wage has been a bipartisan issue and I think it should be again. So I want to challenge you to have honest hearings on this, to get together to find a way to make the minimum wage a living wage.

Members of Congress have been here less than a month but by the end of the week—28 days into the new year—every member of Congress will have earned as much in Congressional salary as a minimum-wage worker makes all year long.

Everybody else here, including the president, has something else that too many Americans do without and that's health care.

Now, last year we almost came to blows over health care, but we didn't do anything. And the cold, hard fact is that since last year—since I was here—another 1.1 million Americans in *working* families have lost their health care. And the cold, hard fact is that many millions more—most of them farmers and small business people and self-employed people—have seen their premiums skyrocket, their co-pays and deductables go up.

There's a whole bunch of people in this country that in the statistics have health insurance but really what they've got is a piece of paper that says they won't lose their home if they get sick.

Now I still believe our country has got to move toward providing health security for every American family, but—but I know that last year, as the evidence indicates, we bit off more than we could chew.

So I'm asking you that we work together. Let's do it step by step. Let's do whatever we have to do to get something done. Let's at least pass meaningful insurance reform so that no American risks losing coverage for facing skyrocketing prices but that nobody loses their coverage because they face high prices or unavailable insurance when they change jobs or lose a job or a family member gets sick.

I want to work together with all of you who have an interest in this: with the Democrats who worked on it last time, with the Republican leaders like Senator Dole who has a longtime commitment to health care reform and made some constructive proposals in this area last year. We ought to make sure that self-employed people in small businesses can buy insurance at more affordable rates through voluntary purchasing pools. We ought to help families provide long-term care for a sick parent to a disabled child. We can work to help workers who lose their jobs at least keep their health insurance coverage for a year while they look for work, and we can find a way—it may take some time, but we can find a way—to make sure that our children have health care.

You know, I think everybody in this room, without regard to party, can be proud of the fact that our country was rated as having the world's most productive economy for the first time in nearly a decade, but we can't be proud of the fact that we're the only wealthy country in the world that has a smaller percentage of the work force and their children with health insurance today than we did 10 years ago—the last time we were the most productive economy in the world.

So let's work together on this. It is too important for politics as usual.

Much of what the American people are thinking about tonight is what we've already talked about. A lot of people think that the security concerns of America today are entirely internal to our borders, they relate to the security of our jobs and our homes and our incomes and our children, our streets, our health and protecting those borders.

Now that the cold war has passed, it's tempting to believe that all the security issues, with the possible exception of trade, reside here at home. But it's not so. Our security still depends on our continued world leadership for peace and freedom and democracy. We still can't be strong at home unless we're strong abroad.

The financial crisis in Mexico is a case in point. I know it's not popular to say it tonight but we have to act, not for the Mexican people but for the sake of the millions of Americans whose livelihoods are tied to Mexico's well-being. If we want to secure American jobs, preserve American exports, safeguard America's borders then we must pass the stabilization program and help to put Mexico back on track.

Now let me repeat: it's not a loan, it's not foreign aid, it's not a bail-out. We'll be given a guarantee like co-signing a note with good collateral that will cover our risk.

This legislation is the right thing for America. That's why the bipartisan leadership has supported it. And I hope you in Congress will pass it quickly. It is in our interest and we can explain it to the American people, because we're going to do it in the right way.

You know, tonight this is the first State of the Union address ever delivered since the beginning of the cold war when not a single Russian missile is pointed at the children of America.

And along with the Russians, we're on our way to destroying the missiles and the bombers that carry 9,000 nuclear warheads. We've come so far so fast in this post-cold-war world that it's easy to take the decline of the nuclear threat for granted. But it's still there, and we aren't finished yet.

This year, I'll ask the Senate to approve START II to eliminate weapons that carry 5,000 more warheads. The United States will lead the charge to extend indefinitely the Nuclear Nonproliferation Treaty, to enact a comprehensive nuclear test ban, and to eliminate chemical weapons.

To stop and roll back North Korea's potentially deadly nuclear program, we'll continue to implement the agreement we have reached with that nation. It's smart, it's tough, it's a deal based on continuing inspection with safeguards for our allies and ourselves.

This year, I'll submit to Congress comprehensive legislation to strengthen our hand in combating terrorists, whether they strike at home or abroad. As the cowards who bombed the World Trade Center found out, this country will hunt down terrorists and bring them to justice.

Just this week, another horrendous terrorist act in Israel killed 19 and injured scores more. On behalf of the American people and all of you, I send our deepest sympathy to the families of the victims. I know that in the face of such evil, it is hard for the people in the Middle East to go forward. But the terrorists represent the past, not the future. We must and we will pursue a comprehensive peace between Israel and all her neighbors in the Middle East.

Accordingly, last night I signed an executive order that will block the assets in the United States of terrorist organizations that threaten to disrupt the peace process. It prohibits financial transactions with these groups.

And tonight I call on all our allies in peace-loving nations throughout the world to join us with renewed fervor in a global effort to combat terrorism, we cannot permit the future to be marred by terror and fear and paralysis.

From the day I took the oath of office, I pledged that our nation would maintain the best-equipped, best-trained and best-prepared military on earth. We have and they are. They have managed the dramatic downsizing of our forces after the cold war with remarkable skill and spirit. But to make sure our military is ready for action and to provide the pay and the quality of life the military and their families deserve, I'm asking the Congress to add $25 billion in defense spending over the next six years.

I have visited many bases at home and around the world since I became President. Tonight I repeat that request with renewed conviction. We ask a very great deal of our armed forces. Now that they are smaller in number, we ask more of them. They go out more often to more different places and stay longer. They are called to service in many, many ways, and we must give them and their families what the times demand and what they have earned.

Just think about what our troops have done in the last year, showing America at its best, helping to save hundreds of thousands of people in Rwanda, moving with lightning speed to head off another threat to Kuwait, giving freedom and democracy back to the people of Haiti.

We have proudly supported peace and prosperity and freedom from South Africa to Northern Ireland, from Central and Eastern Europe to Asia, from Latin America to the Middle East. All these endeavors are good in those places but they make our future more confident and more secure.

Well, my fellow Americans, that's my agenda for America's future: expanding opportunity not bureaucracy, enhancing security at home and abroad, empowering our people to make the most of their own lives.

It's ambitious and achievable. But it's not enough.

We even need more than new ideas for changing the world or equipping Americans to compete in the new economy, more than a government that's smaller, smarter and wiser, more than all the changes we can make in government and in the private sector from the outside in.

Our fortunes and our prosperity also depend upon our ability to answer some questions from within—from the values and voices that speak to our hearts as well as our heads, voices that tell us we have to do more to accept responsibility for ourselves and our families, for our communities, and yes, for our fellow citizens.

We see our families and our communities all over this country coming apart. And we feel the common ground shifting from under us. The P.T.A., the town hall meeting, the ball park—it's hard for a lot of overworked parents to find the time and space for those things that strengthen the bonds of trust and cooperation.

Too many of our children don't even have parents and grandparents who can give them those experiences that they need to build their own character and their sense of identity. We all know that while we here in this chamber can make a difference on those things, that the real difference will be made by our fellow citizens where they work and where they live.

And it'll be made almost without regard to party. When I used to go to the softball park in Little Rock to watch my daughter's league and people would come up to me—fathers and mothers—and talk to me, I can honestly say I had no idea whether 90 percent of them were Republicans or Democrats.

When I visited the relief centers after the floods in California, Northern California, last week, a woman came up to me and did something that very few of you would do. She hugged me and said, "Mr. President, I'm a Republican, but I'm glad you're here."

Now why? We can't wait for disasters to act the way we used to act every day. Because as we move into the next century, everybody matters. We don't have a person to waste. And a lot of people are losing a lot of chances to do better.

That means that we need a New Covenant for everybody—for our corporate and business leaders, we're going to work here to keep bringing the deficit down, to expand markets, to support their success in every possible way. But they have an obligation: when they're doing well, to keep jobs in our communities and give their workers a fair share of the prosperity they generate.

For people in the entertainment industry in this country, we applaud your creativity and your worldwide success and we support your freedom of expression but you do have a responsibility to assess the impact of your work and to understand the damage that comes from the incessant, repetitive, mindless violence and irresponsible conduct that permeates our media all the time.

We've got to ask our community leaders and all kinds of organizations to help us stop our most serious social problem: the epidemic of teen pregnancies and births where there is no marriage. I have sent to Congress a plan to target schools all over this country with anti-pregnancy programs that work. But government can only do so much. Tonight, I call on parents and leaders all across the country to join together in a national campaign against teen pregnancy to make a difference. We can do this and we must.

And I would like to say a special word to our religious leaders. You know, I'm proud of the fact that the United States has more houses of worship per capita than any country in the world. These people, who lead our houses of worship, can ignite their congregations to carry their faith into action, can reach out to all of our children, to all of the people in distress, to those who have been savaged by the breakdown of all we hold dear, because so much of what must be done must come from the inside out. And our religious leaders and their congregations can make all the difference. They have a role in the New Covenant as well.

There must be more responsibility for all of our citizens. You know it takes a lot of people to help all the kids in trouble stay off the streets and in school. It takes a lot of people to build the Habitat for Humanity houses that the Speaker celebrates on his lapel pin. It takes a lot of people to provide the people power for all the civic organizations in this country that made our communities mean so much to most of us when we were kids. It takes every parent to teach the children the difference between right and wrong and to encourage them to learn and grow and say no to the wrong things but also to believe that they can be whatever they want to be.

I know it's hard when you're working harder for less, when you're under great stress, to do these things. A lot of our people don't have the time or emotional stress they think to do the work of citizenship. Most of us in politics haven't helped very much. For years, we've mostly treated citizens like they were consumers or spectators, sort of political couch potatoes who were supposed to watch the TV ads—either promise them something for nothing or play on their fears and frustrations. And more and more of our citizens now get most of their information in very negative and aggressive ways that is hardly conducive to honest and open conversations. But the truth is we have got to stop seeing each other as enemies just because we have different views.

If you go back to the beginning of this country, the great strength of America, as de Tocqueville pointed out when he came here a long time ago, has always been our ability to associate with people who were different from ourselves and to work together to find common ground. And in this day everybody has a responsibility to do more of that. We simply cannot wait for a tornado, a fire or a flood to behave like Americans ought to behave in dealing with one another.

I want to finish up here by pointing out some folks that are up with the First Lady that represent what I'm trying to talk about. Citizens. I have no idea what their party affiliation is or who they voted for in the last election, but they represent what we ought to be doing.

Cindy Perry teaches second-graders to read in Americorps in rural Kentucky. She gains when she gives. She's a mother of four.

She says that her service inspired her to get her high school equivalency last year. She was married when she was a teen-ager. Stand up, Cindy. She married when she was a teen-ager. She had four children, but she had time to serve other people, to get her high school equivalency and she's going to use her Americorps money to go back to college.

Steven Bishop is the police chief of Kansas City. He's been a national leader—stand up Steve. He's been a national leader in using more police in community policing and he's worked with Americorps to do it, and the crime rate in Kansas City has gone down as a result of what he did.

Col. Gregory Depestre went to Haiti as part of his adopted country's force to help secure democracy in his native land. And I might add we must be the only country in the world that could have gone to Haiti and taken Haitian-Americans there who could speak the language and talk to the people, and he was one of them and we're proud of him.

The next two folks I've had the honor of meeting and getting to know a little bit. The Rev. John and the Rev. Diana Cherry of the A.M.E. Zion Church in Temple Hills, Md. I'd like to ask them to stand. I want to tell you about them. In the early 80's they left government service and formed a church in a small living room in a small house in the early 80's. Today that church has 17,000 members. It is one of the three or four biggest churches in the entire United States. It grows by 200 a month.

They do it together. And the special focus of their ministry is keeping families together. There are—Two things that did make a big impression on me. I visited their church once and I learned they were building a new sanctuary closer to the Washington, D.C., line, in a higher-crime, higher-drug-rate area because they thought it was part of their ministry to change the lives of the people who needed them. Second thing I want to say is that once Reverend Cherry was at a meeting at the White House with some other religious leaders and he left early to go back to his church to minister to 150 couples that he had brought back to his church from all over America to convince them to come back together to save their marriages and to raise their kids. This is the kind of work that citizens are doing in America. We need more of it and it ought to be lifted up and supported.

The last person I want to introduce is Jack Lucas from Hattiesburg, Mississippi. Jack, would you stand up. Fifty years ago in the sands of Iwo Jima, Jack Lucas taught and learned the lessons of citizenship. On February the 20th, 1945, he and three of his buddies encountered the enemy and two grenades at their feet. Jack Lucas threw himself on both of them. In that moment he saved the lives of his companions and miraculously in the next instant a medic saved his life. He gained a foothold for freedom and at the age of 17, just a year older than his grandson, who's up there with him today, and his son, who is a West Point graduate and a veteran, at 17, Jack Lucas became the youngest marine in history and the youngest soldier in this century to win the Congressional Medal of Honor. All these years later, yesterday, here's what he said about that day: Didn't matter where you were from or who you were. You relied on one another. You did it for your country. We all gain when we give and we reap what we sow. That's at the heart of this New Covenant. Responsibility, opportunity and citizenship.

More than stale chapters in some remote civic book they're still the virtue by which we can fulfill ourselves and reach our God-given potential and be like them. And also to fulfill the eternal promise of this country, the enduring dream from that first and most-sacred covenant. I believe every person in this country still believes that we are created equal and given by our creator the right to life, liberty and the pursuit of happiness.

This is a very, very great country and our best days are still to come.

Thank you and God bless you all.

---

## A CONTRACT WITH AMERICA[1]
### Newton L. Gingrich[2]

---

The convening of the 104th United States Congress on January 4, 1995, was a historic day for Republicans because for the

[1]Delivered to the United States Congress in the House of Representatives in Washington, D.C. on January 4, 1995 at 2:00 p.m.
[2]For biographical note see Appendix.

first time in forty years their party had majorities in both the House of Representatives and the Senate. Leadership in the two Houses had changed from Democratic hands to Republican. Both new majority leaders—Newt Gingrich in the House and Bob Dole in the Senate—began their respective sessions with speeches outlining their plans and hopes for the new Congress.

Public interest in the two speeches was high. Voters in the 1994 elections had clearly rejected Democratic leadership of Congress. Now they wished to learn what the Republicans hoped to accomplish.

In his address at the opening of the House session, the new Majority Leader, Newt Gingrich of Georgia, made an appeal for bipartisan unity, but clearly the main purpose of the speech was to outline the major objectives of the Republicans. These had been set forth in a document called "A Contract With America" prepared by the party before the November elections. Gingrich's speech highlighted the aims of the Republicans as proposed in the Contract.

*Representative Gingrich's speech:* We are starting the 104th Congress. I do not know if you have ever thought about this, but for 208 years, we bring together the most diverse country in the history of the world. We send all sorts of people here. Each of us could find at least one Member we thought was weird. I will tell you, if you went around the room the person chosen to be weird would be different for virtually every one of us. Because we do allow and insist upon the right of a free people to send an extraordinary diversity of people here.

Brian Lamb of C-SPAN read to me Friday a phrase from de Tocqueville that was so central to the House. I have been reading Remini's biography of Henry Clay and Clay, as the first strong Speaker, always preferred the House. He preferred the House to the Senate although he served in both. He said the House is more vital, more active, more dynamic, and more common.

This is what de Tocqueville wrote:

"Often there is not a distinguished man in the whole number. Its members are almost all obscure individuals whose names bring no associations to mind. They are mostly village lawyers, men in trade, or even persons belonging to the lower classes of society."

If we include women, I do not know that we would change much. But the word "vulgar" in de Tocqueville's time had a very particular meaning. It is a meaning the world would do well to study in this room. You see, de Tocqueville was an aristocrat. He lived in a world of kings and princes. The folks who come here do so by the one single act that their citizens freely chose them. I do not care what your ethnic background is, or your ideology. I do not care if you are younger or older. I do not care if you are born in America or if you are a naturalized citizen. Every one of the 435 people have equal standing because their citizens freely sent them. Their voice should be heard and they should have a right to participate. It is the most marvelous act of a complex giant country trying to argue and talk. And, as Dick Gephardt said, to have a great debate, to reach great decisions, not through a civil war, not by bombing one of our regional capitals, not by killing a half million people, and not by having snipers. Let me say unequivocally, I condemn all acts of violence against the law by all people for all reasons. This is a society of law and a society of civil behavior.

Here we are as commoners together, to some extent Democrats and Republicans, to some extent liberals and conservatives, but Americans all. Steve Gunderson today gave me a copy of the "Portable Abraham Lincoln." He suggested there is much for me to learn about our party, but I would also say that it does not hurt to have a copy of the portable F.D.R.

This is a great country of great people. If there is any one factor or acts of my life that strikes me as I stand up here as the first Republican in 40 years to do so, is when I first became whip in 1989, Russia was beginning to change, the Soviet Union as it was then. Into my whip's office one day came eight Russians and a Lithuanian, members of the Communist Party, newspaper editors. They asked me, "What does a whip do?"

They said,

"In Russia we have never had a free parliament since 1917 and that was only for a few months, so what do you do?"

I tried to explain, as Dave Bonior or Tom DeLay might now. It is a little strange if you are from a dictatorship to explain you are called the whip but you do not really have a whip, you are elected by the people you are supposed to pressure—other members. If you pressure them too much they will not reelect you. On the other hand if you do not pressure them enough they will not reelect you. Democracy is hard. It is frustrating.

So our group came into the Chamber. The Lithuanian was a man in his late sixties, and I allowed him to come up here and sit and be Speaker, something many of us have done with constituents. Remember, this is the very beginning of perestroika and glasnost. When he came out of the chair, he was physically trembling. He was almost in tears. He said,

"Ever since World War II, I have remembered what the Americans did and I have never believed the propaganda. But I have to tell you, I did not think in my life that I would be able to sit at the center of freedom."

It was one of the most overwhelming, compelling moments of my life. It struck me that something I could not help but think of when we were here with President Mandela. I went over and saw Ron Dellums and thought of the great work Ron had done to extend freedom across the planet. You get that sense of emotion when you see something so totally different than you had expected. Here was a man who reminded me first of all that while presidents are important, they are in effect an elected kingship, that this and the other body across the way are where freedom has to be fought out. That is the tradition I hope that we will take with us as we go to work.

Today we had a bipartisan prayer service. Frank Wolf made some very important points. He said,

"We have to recognize that many of our most painful problems as a country are moral problems, problems of dealing with ourselves and with life."

He said character is the key to leadership and we have to deal with that. He preached a little bit. I do not think he thought he was preaching, but he was. It was about a spirit of reconciliation. He talked about caring about our spouses and our children and our families. If we are not prepared to model our own family life beyond just having them here for one day, if we are not prepared to care about our children and we are not prepared to care about our families, then by what arrogance do we think we will transcend our behavior to care about others? That is why with Congressman Gephardt's help we have established a bipartisan task force on the family. We have established the principle that we are going to set schedules we stick to so families can count on time to be together, built around school schedules so that families can get to know each other, and not just by seeing us on C-SPAN.

I will also say that means one of the strongest recommendations of the bipartisan committee, is that we have 17 minutes to vote. This is the bipartisan committee's recommendations, not just mine. They pointed out that if we take the time we spent in the last Congress where we waited for one more member, and one more, and one more, that we literally can shorten the business and get people home if we will be strict and firm. At one point this year we had a 45-minute vote. I hope all of my colleagues are paying attention because we are in fact going to work very hard to have 17 minute votes and it is over. So, leave on the first bell, not the second bell. Ok? This may seem particularly inappropriate to say on the first day because this will be the busiest day on opening day in congressional history.

I want to read just a part of the Contract With America. I don't mean this as a partisan act, but rather to remind all of us what we are about to go through and why. Those of us who ended up in the majority stood on these steps and signed a contract, and here is part of what it says:

"On the first day of the 104th Congress the new Republican majority will immediately pass the following reforms aimed at restoring the faith and trust of the American people in their government: First, require all laws that apply to the rest of the country also to apply equally to the Congress. Second, select a major, independent auditing firm to conduct a comprehensive audit of the Congress for waste, fraud or abuse. Third, cut the number of House committees and cut committee staffs by a third. Fourth, limit the terms of all committee chairs. Fifth, ban the casting of proxy votes in committees. Sixth, require committee meetings to be open to the public. Seven, require a three-fifths majority vote to pass a tax increase. Eight, guarantee an honest accounting of our federal budget by implementing zero baseline budgeting."

Now, I told Dick Gephardt last night that if I had to do it over again we would have pledged within 3 days that we will do these things, but that is not what we said. So we have ourselves in a little bit of a box here.

Then we go a step further. I carry the T.V. Guide version of the contract with me at all times.

We then say that within the first 100 days of the 104th Congress we shall bring to the House floor the following bills, each to be given full and open debate, each to be given a full and clear vote, and each to be immediately available for inspection. We made it available that day. We listed 10 items. A balanced budget amendment and line-item veto, a bill to stop violent criminals, emphasizing among other things an effective and enforceable death penalty. Third was welfare reform. Fourth, legislation protecting our kids. Fifth was to provide tax cuts for families. Sixth was a bill to strengthen our national defense. Seventh was a bill to raise the senior citizens' earning limit. Eighth was legislation rolling back Government regulations. Ninth was a commonsense legal reform bill, and tenth was congressional term limits legislation.

Our commitment on our side, and this is an absolute obligation, is first of all to work today until we are done. I know that is going to inconvenience people who have families and supporters. But we were hired to do a job, and we have to start today to prove we will do it. Second, I would say to our friends in the Democratic Party that we are going to work with you, and we are really laying out a schedule working with the minority leader to make sure that we can set dates certain to go home. That does mean that if 2 or 3 weeks out we are running short we will, frankly, have longer sessions on Tuesday, Wednesday, and Thursday. We will try to work this out on a bipartisan basis to, in a workmanlike way, get it done. It is going to mean the busiest early months since 1933.

Beyond the Contract I think there are two giant challenges. I know I am a partisan figure. But I really hope today that I can speak for a minute to my friends in the Democratic Party as well as my own colleagues, and speak to the country about these two challenges so that I hope we can have a real dialog. One challenge is to achieve a balanced budget by 2002. I think both Democratic and Republican governors will say we can do that but it is hard. I do not think we can do it in a year or two. I do not think we ought to lie to the American people. This is a huge, complicated job.

The second challenge is to find a way to truly replace the current welfare state with an opportunity society.

Let me talk very briefly about both challenges. First, on the balanced budget I think we can get it done. I think the baby boomers are now old enough that we can have an honest dialog about priorities, about resources, about what works, and what does not work. Let me say I have already told Vice President Gore that we are going to invite him to address a Republican conference. We would have invited him in December but he had to go to Moscow. I believe there are grounds for us to talk together and to work together, to have hearings together, and to have task forces together. If we set priorities, if we apply the principles of Edward Deming and of Peter Drucker we can build on the Vice President's reinventing government effort and we can focus on transforming, not just cutting. The choice becomes not just do you want more or do you want less, but are there ways to do it better? Can we learn from the private sector, can we learn from Ford, IBM, from Microsoft, from what General Motors has had to go through? I think on a bipartisan basis we owe it to our children and grandchildren to get this government in order and to be able to actually pay our way. I think 2002 is a reasonable timeframe. I would hope that together we could open a dialog with the American people.

I have said that I think Social Security ought to be off limits, at least for the first 4 to 6 years of the process, because I think it will just destroy us if we try to bring it into the game. But let me say about everything else, whether it is Medicare, or it is agricultural subsidies, or it is defense or anything that I think the greatest Democratic President of the 20th century, and in my judgment the greatest President of the 20th century, said it right. On March 4, 1933, he stood in braces as a man who had polio at a time when nobody who had that kind of disability could be anything in public life. He was President of the United States, and he stood in front of this Capitol on a rainy March day and he said, "We have nothing to fear but fear itself."

I want every one of us to reach out in that spirit and pledge to live up to that spirit, and I think frankly on a bipartisan basis. I would say to members of the Black and Hispanic Caucuses that I would hope we could arrange by late spring to genuinely share districts. You could have a Republican who frankly may not know a thing about your district agree to come for a long weekend with you, and you will agree to go for a long weekend with them. We begin a dialog and an openness that is totally different than people are used to seeing in politics in America. I believe if we do that we can then create a dialog that can lead to a balanced budget.

But I think we have a greater challenge. I do want to pick up directly on what Dick Gephardt said, because he said it right. No Republican here should kid themselves about it. The greatest leaders in fighting for an integrated America in the 20th century were in the Democratic Party. The fact is, it was the liberal wing of the Democratic Party that ended segregation. The fact is that it was Franklin Delano Roosevelt who gave hope to a Nation that was in distress and could have slid into dictatorship. Every Republican has much to learn from studying what the Democrats did right.

But I would say to my friends in the Democratic Party that there is much to what Ronald Reagan was trying to get done. There is much to what is being done today by Republicans like Bill Weld, and John Engler, and Tommy Thompson, and George Allen, and Christy Whitman, and Pete Wilson. There is much we can share with each other.

We must replace the welfare state with an opportunity society. The balanced budget is the right thing to do. But it does not in my mind have the moral urgency of coming to grips with what is happening to the poorest Americans.

I commend to all Marvin Olasky's "The Tragedy of American Compassion." Olasky goes back for 300 years and looked at what has worked in America, how we have helped people rise beyond poverty, and how we have reached out to save people. He may not have the answers, but he has the right sense of where we have to go as Americans.

I do not believe that there is a single American who can see a news report of a 4-year-old thrown off of a public housing project in Chicago by other children and killed and not feel that a part of your heart went, too. I think of my nephew in the back, Kevin, and how all of us feel about our children. How can any American read about an 11-year-old buried with his teddy bear because he killed a 14-year-old, and then another 14-year-old killed him, and not have some sense of "My God, where has this country gone?" How can we not decide that this is a moral crisis equal to segregation, equal to slavery? How can we not insist that every day we take steps to do something?

I have seldom been more shaken than I was after the election when I had breakfast with two members of the Black Caucus. One of them said to me,

"Can you imagine what it is like to visit a first-grade class and realize that every fourth or fifth young boy in that class may be dead or in jail within 15 years? And they are your constituents and you are helpless to change it?"

For some reason, I do not know why, maybe because I visit a lot of schools, that got through. I mean, that personalized it. That made it real, not just statistics, but real people.

Then I tried to explain part of my thoughts by talking about the need for alternatives to the bureaucracy, and we got into what I think frankly has been a pretty distorted and cheap debate over orphanages.

Let me say, first of all, my father, who is here today, was a foster child. He was adopted as a teenager. I am adopted. We have relatives who were adopted. We are not talking out of some vague impersonal Dickens "Bleak House" middle-class intellectual model. We have lived the alternatives.

I believe when we are told that children are so lost in the city bureaucracies that there are children who end up in dumpsters, when we are told that there are children doomed to go to schools where 70 or 80 percent of them will not graduate, when we are told of public housing projects that are so dangerous that if any private sector ran them they would be put in jail, and the only solution we are given is, "Well, we will study it, we will get around to it," my only point is that this is unacceptable. We can find ways immediately to do things better, to reach out, break through the bureaucracy and give every young American child a better chance.

Let me suggest to you Morris Schectman's new book. I do not agree with all of it, but it is fascinating. It is entitled "Working Without a Net." It is an effort to argue that in the 21st century we have to create our own safety nets. He draws a distinction between caring and caretaking. It is worth every American reading.

He said caretaking is when you bother me a little bit, and I do enough, I feel better because I think I took care of you. That is not any good to you at all. You may be in fact an alcoholic and I just gave you the money to buy the bottle that kills you, but I feel better and go home. He said caring is actually stopping and dealing with the human being, trying to understand enough about them to genuinely make sure you improve their life, even if you have to start with a conversation like, "If you will quit drinking, I will help you get a job." This is a lot harder conversation than, "I feel better. I gave him a buck or 5 bucks."

I want to commend every member on both sides to look carefully. I say to those Republicans who believe in total privatization, you cannot believe in the Good Samaritan and explain that as long as business is making money we can walk by a fellow American who is hurt and not do something. I would say to my friends on the left who believe there has never been a government program that was not worth keeping, you cannot look at some of the results we now have and not want to reach out to the humans and forget the bureaucracies.

If we could build that attitude on both sides of this aisle, we would be an amazingly different place, and the country would begin to be a different place.

We have to create a partnership. We have to reach out to the American people. We are going to do a lot of important things. Thanks to the House Information System and Congressman Vern Ehlers, as of today we are going to be on line for the whole country, every amendment, every conference report. We are working with C-SPAN and others, and Congressman Gephardt has agreed to help on a bipartisan basis to make the building more open to television, more accessible to the American people. We have talk radio hosts here today for the first time. I hope to have a bipartisan effort to make the place accessible for all talk radio hosts of all backgrounds, no matter their ideology. The House Historian's office is going to be more aggressively run on a bipartisan basis to reach out to Close Up, and to other groups to teach what the legislative struggle is about. I think over time we can and will this Spring rethink campaign reform and lobbying reform and review all ethics, including the gift rule.

But that isn't enough. Our challenge shouldn't be just to balance the budget or to pass the Contract. Our challenge should not be anything that is just legislative. We are supposed to, each one of us, be leaders. I think our challenge has to be to set as our goal, and maybe we are not going to get there in 2 years. This ought to be the goal that we go home and we tell people we believe in: that there will be a Monday morning when for the entire weekend not a single child was killed anywhere in America; that there will be a Monday morning when every child in the country went to a school that they and their parents thought prepared them as citizens and prepared them to compete in the world market; that there will be a Monday morning where it was easy to find a job or create a job, and your own government did not punish you if you tried.

We should not be happy just with the language of politicians and the language of legislation. We should insist that our success for America is felt in the neighborhoods, in the communities, is felt by real people living real lives who can say, "Yes we are safer, we are healthier, we are better educated, America succeeds."

This morning's closing hymn at the prayer service was the Battle Hymn of the Republic. It is hard to be in this building, look down past Grant to the Lincoln Memorial and not realize how painful and how difficult that battle hymn is. The key phrase is, "As he died to make men holy, let us live to make men free."

It is not just political freedom, although I agree with everything Congressman Gephardt said earlier. If you cannot afford to leave the public housing project, you are not free. If you do not know how to find a job and do not know how to create a job, you are not free. If you cannot find a place that will educate you, you are not free. If you are afraid to walk to the store because you could get killed, you are not free.

So as all of us over the coming months sing that song, "As he died to make men holy, let us live to make men free," I want us to dedicate ourselves to reach out in a genuinely non-partisan way to be honest with each other. I promise each of you that without regard to party my door is going to be open. I will listen to each of you. I will try to work with each of you. I will put in long hours, and I will guarantee that I will listen to you first. I will let you get it all out before I give you my version, because you have been patient with me today, and you have given me a chance to set the stage.

But I want to close by reminding all of us of how much bigger this is than us. Because beyond talking with the American people, beyond working together, I think we can only be successful if we start with our limits. I was very struck this morning with something Bill Emerson used, a very famous quote of Benjamin Franklin, at the point where the Constitutional Convention was deadlocked. People were tired, and there was a real possibility that the Convention was going to break up. Franklin, who was quite old and had been relatively quiet for the entire Convention, suddenly stood up and was angry, and he said:

> "I have lived, sir, a long time, and the longer I live the more convincing proofs I see of this truth, that God governs in the affairs of men, and if a sparrow cannot fall to the ground without His notice, is it possible that an empire can rise without His aid?"

At that point the Constitutional Convention stopped. They took a day off for fasting and prayer.

Then, having stopped and come together, they went back, and they solved the great question of large and small States. They wrote the Constitution, and the United States was created. All I can do is pledge to you that, if each of us will reach out prayerfully and try to genuinely understand each other, if we will recognize that in this building we symbolize America, and that we have an obligation to talk with each other, then I think a year from now we can look on the 104th Congress as a truly amazing institution without regard to party, without regard to ideology. We can say, "Here, America comes to work, and here we are preparing for those children a better future."

Thank you. Good luck and God bless you.

## COMMITMENT TO VALUES[1]
### EDWARD M. KENNEDY[2]

The victories in the November 1994 Congressional elections, which gave Republicans control of both the United States senate and House of Representatives for the first time in 40 years, led many Democratic politicians to reexamine their policies and positions in relation to the country and their constituencies. A small number of Democrats in Congress switched to the Republican Party and a few, for various reasons, decided not to stand for reelection.

One leader who spoke out in support of traditional Democratic liberal policies in spite of the election results was Senator Edward M. Kennedy of Massachusetts. Kennedy, who had turned what seemed to be a very close race for reelection into a landslide victory in the fall election, addressed the National Press Club on January 14, 1995, in his first major speech since his reelection.

Kennedy, described by Adam Clymer as "The Senate's leading liberal in a conservative age" (*New York Times,* January 15, 1995) said, "We are, without apology, the party that believes in assisting the poor and the disabled and the disadvantaged, but not to the detriment of the hard-working middle class."

The National Press Club in Washington, D.C., provides an excellent forum for speakers seeking media coverage of their ideas. The club sponsors regular breakfast, luncheon, and dinner sessions as part of a series to which prominent public figures are invited to speak on important issues. Since most of the audience are members of the media—local, national, and international—the speakers' remarks often receive widespread attention.

*Senator Kennedy's speech:* I come here as a Democrat. I reject such qualifiers as New Democrat or Old Democrat or Neo-Democrat. I am committed to the enduring principles of the Democratic Party, and I am proud of its great tradition of service to the people who are the heart and strength of this nation—working families and the middle class.

[1]Delivered to the National Press Club, in the ballroom of the National Press Club in Washington, D.C. on January 11, 1995 at 1:00 p.m.
[2]For biographical note, see Appendix.

I would have lost in Massachusetts if I had done what Democrats who were defeated in other parts of the country too often tried to do.

I was behind in mid-September. But I believe I won because I ran for health reform, not away from it. I ran for a minimum wage increase, not against it. I continued to talk about issues like jobs, aid to education, and job training. And I attacked Republican proposals to tilt the tax code to the most privileged of our people.

I stood against limiting welfare benefits if a mother has another child, and I will stand against any other harsh proposals that aim at the mother but hit and hurt innocent children. I spoke out for gun control, and against reactionary Republican proposals to abandon crime prevention as a weapon in the war on crime. I rejected the Republican double standard that welcomes government as benign when it subsidizes the affluent, but condemns government as the enemy when it helps the poor.

I ran as a Democrat in belief as well as name. This turned out to be not only right in principle—it was also the best politics.

I talked about the issues that mattered to working families, and about what I had tried to do to address their needs and concerns. I take some sense of pride and satisfaction that exit polling showed 89 percent of Massachusetts voters—by far the highest percentage in the country—said they had learned enough about the candidates and the issues in the Senate race to make an informed choice.

Our issues, if we defend them, are popular. The working families in New Bedford, Fall River, Lowell, Lawrence, Springfield and Worcester in my state voted for me, and they have the same concerns as working families throughout the country.

The caricatures of us by the other side will be ineffective—as long as we vigorously oppose them and expose them, instead of sheepishly acquiescing them. If Democrats run for cover, if we become pale carbon copies of the opposition and try to act like Republicans, we will lose—and deserve to lose. As I have said on other occasions, Democrats must be more than warmed-over Republicans. The last thing this country needs is two Republican parties.

If we fall for our opponents' tactics, if we listen to those who tell us to abandon health reform or slash student loans and children's programs, or engage in a bidding war to see who can be the most anti-government or the most laissez-faire, we will have only ourselves to blame. As Democrats, we can win, but only if we stand for something.

The election last November was not a ratification of Republican solutions. By the narrowest of margins, they gained control of Congress. But less than 40 percent of eligible voters turned out on election day, and only slightly more than half of those—about 20 percent—cast ballots for Republicans. Some mandate!

As the current controversy over the motor voter law demonstrates, Republicans thrive by depressing voter turnout. Intensity matters for Democrats. Turnout will certainly be higher in 1996—fifty or sixty percent higher. We must stand our Democratic ground. We must fight for the ideals that are the very reason for our party's being. We must prove to working families and average citizens that we are on their side, fighting hard for them. If we do, then Democrats will turn out and come home in 1996. The defeat of 1994 will be history, and we will be back, stronger than ever—not stale from the past, but renewed for the future.

But to achieve that victory, we must not repeat the mistakes of the past. We must make explicit to the American people our core values and beliefs which form the basis of our political philosophy and underlie our legislative proposals—specifically and most important, that we as Americans, with all our diversity, share a common purpose, a common sense of family, neighborhood, community, and country, of fairness, responsibility, and decency.

Unfortunately, we have failed in the past to make these vital and important points as clearly as we should. We Democrats have always considered family, community, faith and love of country to be core values—the foundation upon which all of our proposals are based. But we allowed Republicans to take these values as their own. We assumed too quickly that our commitment to such values was self-evident in the proposals we made and the legislation we passed. We were wrong, and we paid a price because of it.

So let me set the record straight. Family, community, love of country, fairness, responsibility—all of these values underlie the philosophy of the Democratic Party. And these are the values that underlie and must underlie all of our legislative proposals.

This is not to say, however, that I believe these core values should be used as a superficial rationale for bumper sticker solutions to the complex problems we face. No, these core values require us to reject simple, easy answers which may make us feel good today, but do absolutely nothing to solve these problems. Our values oblige us to address these problems in a thoughtful and productive way.

We are, without apology, the party that believes in assisting the poor and the disabled and the disadvantaged—but not to the detriment of the hard-working middle class, which is justifiably frustrated and angry. They feel left out and left behind, because they know they are losing ground. They see the wealthiest Americans becoming wealthier. They see the poorest Americans being taken care of by society's safety net—which their tax dollars have put in place.

Americans are angry, and rightly so. Rapid economic change and surging global competition have made many jobs and people less secure. The vast majority of Americans are working harder and making less. Yet fair reward for work has always been essential to their hope of creating better lives for their families and their children.

As Democrats, we must address that anger and frustration. But the answer is not to create larger problems by dismantling the safety net, leaving the poor to fend for themselves. Such a result is not only inhumane, it is wrong and destructive to our country, our communities, and our values.

Nor is the solution to give more tax breaks to the wealthiest Americans, in the hope that something will trickle down to the middle class. This country was founded on equal opportunity for all, not unequal opportunity for some.

Instead, we must be more responsive and give a greater helping hand to working families and the middle class. In this central battle for their minds and hearts, heritage and history are on our side. Recall the great victorious battles of the past—for Social Security and Medicare, for the minimum wage and the rights of workers, for civil rights and equal rights, for protection of the environment, for a Head Start for every child and the education of all children regardless of their parents' income, for family and medical leave, for opportunity for women and a woman's right to choose. By any standard, these were extraordinary achievements. And all of them were won because they were sought and fought for by members of the Democratic Party.

Let us not forget that many of these measures, which the American people now accept as part of our way of life, were opposed at the time by the majority of Republicans in Congress. Democrats bled—and suffered lasting battle scars for these victories. But there are few if any Republicans who would refight them or repeal them now.

These historic victories strengthened families, strengthened communities, and brought Americans together. They reflect the fundamental dedication of the Democratic Party to a sense of progress that embraces all Americans. Our achievements remind us of our roots, inspire us to fight harder now, and give us a credibility and a vision that history denies Republicans in fighting for the future.

Surely, the challenges we face in the 1990's are no greater than those we faced in other years. People want government to be more responsive to their problems and more effective in resolving them. I'm talking about basic things that make a difference in people's lives. A strong growing economy. A clear commitment to keep the current recovery going, and to keep the deficit heading down. Good jobs and decent wages where hard work pays off in rising standards of living, not falling farther behind. Safe streets and neighborhoods. Schools that give students a good education. Child care and health care that are accessible and affordable to all. Rekindling the sense of community and patriotism, of shared values and individual responsibility, of service to others—to neighborhoods and the nation alike.

These ideals are, have always been, and must continue to be our Democratic priorities. And we made more progress on them in the last two years than most voters ever knew on election day.

But there is no profit in endlessly regretting the denial of credit to President Clinton and the Democratic Party for a remarkable record of achievement.

One reason for the lack of credit is that the President and the Democratic Congress took on an almost unprecedented array of tough challenges, and did not win every battle. Another reason is that we live in a period of vast economic and social transformation, in which the politics of fear is easily marshaled to overrun the politics of hope.

And another reason, I am convinced, is a Republican strategy of obstruction, distortion, and massive personal attack on the President and the First Lady. In the wake of this election, Democrats need to fight back for our beliefs, not turn our back on the Clinton Administration.

Blaming Bill Clinton by some in our party comes with ill grace from those who abandoned him on critical votes in the last Congress, then ran from him in the campaign—and then lost, often by wide margins. Now they come forward to advocate a strategy discredited by their own defeats.

My fundamental recommendation to the President is that he stay the course of change and do what he thinks is right. My advice to my fellow Democrats is that we work with the President for change—instead of seeking to change our principles, or distance ourselves from him.

No one wants a repeat of the Republican tactic in 1994 that made the "G" in G.O.P. stand for gridlock. We must try to reach across party lines—and build bipartisan coalitions to do the things the nation needs and deserves. This is an obligation on both sides, Republicans as well as Democrats. We must never forget that it takes two parties to be bipartisan.

I believe in free enterprise—but I believe in active government too. A practical way to blend them both and make government more effective is through what I have called public enterprise— using market forces wherever possible, not asking taxpayers to blindly pay for programs, but insisting that programs be genuine investments in a brighter future, and produce results commensurate with their cost.

There is no doubt that many programs are not successful. A federal program is not the solution to every problem. But there continues to be an important federal role in solving the problems of our society by investing in people and the infrastructure needed for our country to succeed and our citizens to thrive. To believe otherwise is hostile to the basic values of our country and to the historic concept of "We the People" in our Constitution. We must not rob the people of the resource of government. It is their government, and we must make it work for them.

We do need to streamline government and make it more responsive to average Americans. But as President Clinton said last month, people want government to be lean, not mean. There is a large difference between reinventing government and rejecting it—and an even larger difference between using government to promote the general welfare and misusing it to pander to the powerful and punish the powerless.

If we keep these truths in mind, we can find real solutions that work for health care, schools, and jobs, and achieve a rising standard of living for all. We can deal effectively with crime, welfare, race, and immigration—instead of allowing our opponents to keep on welding grievances, anger, suspicion, and even outright bigotry into weapons of mass destruction for their next campaigns.

Democrats can win the current debate on the budget and on tax relief for the middle class. Republicans can disguise their intentions all they want. But the heart of the Republican plan are deep reductions in Medicare and Medicaid, and lavish tax cuts that favor the wealthy—especially their capital gains tax cut, the classic Republican tax break for the rich—trickle down economics at its worst. That is not what the 1994 elections were about, and the Republicans and the voters know it.

We must also resist our opponents' mindless anti-government vendetta against regulation—a rhetoric leading to an across-the-board assault on government that hides a multitude of injustices and indifferences.

Republicans wanted to get government out of the savings and loan industry in the worst way in the 1980s—and they did. Deregulation ran amuck. The S & L mess became one of the most serious scandals in our history, costing taxpayers more than a hundred and fifty billion dollars.

So my advice to Republicans is to make sure there is water in the pool before they leap off their pro-business anti-regulation diving board. Government is there for a reason—to help people, including the middle class.

There are mounting needs and frustrations in this land. But it will only make things worse, not better, to shred the safety net, or deregulate health and safety. Nostalgia for a past that never was is not a policy for the future.

Where do we go from here? Let me outline some key priorities that should be part of our Democratic agenda for 1995, because they are part of our strategy to strengthen and invest in the community we call America.

No issue better represents the commitment of the Democratic Party to strengthen families and communities than the drive for comprehensive health reform. It is a total misreading of the election—and a deliberate misreading of the public will—to conclude this issue is no longer important or urgent.

For some in Congress, with their blue chip coverage under the federal government plan, health reform may be only a political game, where points are won or lost. But to the majority of Americans, it is a continuing worsening problem, where their health, their children and their family, their financial security, and often their very lives are at stake.

The real value of the average working family paycheck has been stagnant for many years, but the share that goes for health has soared. Excessive inflation in health costs means less and less of the paycheck is available for everything else. Millions of working men and women risk losing the insurance they have, if they change or lose their job. And for too many senior citizens and persons with disabilities, the high cost of prescription drugs and long term care has broken the promise of Social Security and Medicare.

Democrats fought for health reform in the last Congress, but we did not fight well. We made serious mistakes that contributed to our failure. But I am certain that in large part we were defeated because of the cynical Republican calculation that successful health reform would benefit Democrats at the polls and thwart Republican election goals. And so they settled on a strategy of relentless obstruction.

No one can know for sure. But I believe voters would have rallied to Democrats in 1994 if we had gone down fighting as hard as we could for health reform. Instead, we engaged in a search for a phantom compromise that our opponents never intended to achieve. We allowed the great debate in Congress to end without a vote—with a whimper, not a bang—and we must not make that mistake again.

Now, Republicans have had their election—and their victory. I ask them—and challenge them—to join us in fashioning a health bill and enacting it into law in 1995. Sit down with us for real. Get serious about coming to agreement. Bring Harry and Louise if you like—but let's expose special interest pleading for what it is. Shape a compromise that deals realistically with the problem, rather than treating each offer of compromise as a pretext for new demands—which is what happened last year.

It would be nice if the Republican Contract with America contained even a hint of this simple pledge—to give every American the same health care that the newly-elected signers of the Contract are receiving from the federal government. We are now making Congress abide by the same laws we pass for others. Why not give the American people the benefit of the same laws that Congress passes for itself?

A second major challenge, if we are serious about revitalizing our communities and investing in families and the nation's future, is reform in job education.

Today we have scores of separate job training programs costing billions of dollars a year—and workers are not getting their money's worth. President Clinton and the Democratic Leadership Council are right to call for vouchers and greater reliance on market forces, so that workers can circumvent the bureaucracy and choose the training they want.

We must also focus more on outcomes. Too often, the path of least resistance has been to create more and more training programs—without the follow-through to see that they succeed in actually preparing people for jobs and placing them in jobs. We must reward those that are successful—and de-fund those that fall short.

We must do more to redress the widening gap between soaring profits and stagnant wages. We must insist that firms provide training for their workers. I make no apology for supporting a mandate in an area like this. Often, a mandate is the only practical way to assure that free enterprise is fair as well as free. Through the minimum wage, we ask business to invest in the lowest paid workers, and the time has come to ask business to invest in all workers by providing a minimum level of training.

Companies make choices. Some firms train their workers well, upgrade their skills, and offer good benefits. They treat workers as valuable resources, and still earn good profits. Other companies rely on a harsher strategy that exploits workers. They downsize. They lay off good workers. They hire part-time employees to avoid paying benefits. They cut corners on safety.

Congress should do more, not less, to encourage companies to do the right thing and prevent unfair competition from those that don't. Mandates make sense in areas like job training and health care. We must break the iron grip of a Gresham's Law of Business, in which irresponsible firms drive out firms attempting to be responsible.

A third major challenge to invest in our future and strengthen our American community relates to education. With college costs rising—over $8,000 a year at many public universities and over $20,000 at many private colleges—the American dream is too often an impossible dream for many families.

Let's hold the line against even one cent of Republican cuts in college aid. How dare anyone offer a Contract with America that professes allegiance to the middle class, but that would slam college doors in the face of their children. Basic values are at stake. Let's strengthen the Department of Education not abolish it. Let's oppose and defeat education cuts that would be nothing more than federal aid for ignorance.

Finally, a top priority for this Congress is reform of the lobbying and campaign finance laws. No change will do more to strengthen our American community and make greater progress possible on every other issue than breaking the stranglehold of special interest groups and restoring government that truly represents "We the People."

We must end the power of special interest money and political action committees, and take elections off the auction block. We must make lobbyists disclose what they're doing in the back rooms to subvert the public interest. It is time to end the lavish gifts, meals, entertainment and expensive trips paid for by special interests.

A sunshine law for lobbyists will pay a dividend to you in the press as well, because it will enable you to expose what really happens in the ongoing battles between the special interests and the public interest.

These are major items on a Democratic agenda for recovery in 1995. But in a larger sense, they are at the heart of a constructive and needed American agenda to restore the sense of family and community, of caring for one another, and of building a brighter future that will once again reflect this nation at its best.

In all this, we must understand that sometimes the task of a great political party is to face the tide—not just ride with it—and to turn it again in the direction of our deepest convictions. We will lose our way—and our elections—if we abandon our principles and drift with the shifting politics of the moment.

Let's renew our cause as Democrats. Let's hold our standard high and advance it proudly. Let's be who we are, and not pretend to be something else. And if we do, we will have a strong and winning case to take to the American people in this new Congress and in all the years ahead. The Republican majority will be a transient one, and the Democrats will be proud to be Democrats again.

---

## A FAREWELL TO PUBLIC OFFICE[1]
### MARIO M. CUOMO[2]

Among the many Democratic casualties in the November, 1994, Republican landslide victory was Governor Mario M. Cuomo of New York, who lost to a virtually unknown challenger George E. Pataki. Cuomo, who had served as governor for three terms and was widely regarded as one of the Democratic Party's outstanding orators, had frequently been urged, but always refused, to stand for the party's nomination for president.

[1]Delivered to the National Press Club, Washington, D.C., on December 16, 1994.
[2]For biographical note see Appendix.

His defeat for reelection to a fourth term came as a surprise to most political observers. On December 16, 1994, at the National Press Club in Washington, D.C. Cuomo delivered what he said would be his last speech as a public official. The National Press Club provides one of the best forums for speakers to make their views known not only in the capital but also throughout the country and around the world. The club, headquarters for reporters, media representatives from all the major newspapers, news agencies, radio and television networks, sponsors a series of breakfast, luncheon, and dinner lectures where prominent speakers may air their views.

Governor Cuomo delivered his thirty-five-minute address to an audience of reporters, politicians, and interested spectators. It was reprinted in the *Congressional Record* and widely covered by the national media.

Melinda Henneberger, writing in the *New York Times,* reported that Cuomo began "by excusing himself for talking so fast. There was so much he wanted to say." He discussed his future plans, denying reports that he might become a Supreme Court Justice, commissioner of baseball, or chairman of the Democratic National Committee, and instead suggested other directions his career might take. "Of yesterday's speech," Henneberger reported:

> Mr. Cuomo said it was so short that it left out "a lot of good stuff." In it, he was wholly unapologetic and combative as ever, calling Republican proposals to simultaneously cut taxes, boost military spending and balance the budget "deja voodoo." (*New York Times,* December 17, 1994, p. 16)

Two weeks later, Cuomo spent his last day in Albany as Governor of New York, Kevin Sack observed:

> Mario M. Cuomo left the Governor's office today as he arrived twelve years ago, delivering a valedictory homily about the "family of New York" and displaying the contradictory impulses that made him both the most inspiring and most exasperating of state leaders. (*New York Times,* December 31, 1994, p. 31)

*Governor Cuomo's speech:* Thank you very much. Thank you very much. There are a lot of things I wanted to say immediately, just in quick response to Gil Klein's introduction. I—the truth about 1992 was that Klein, or somebody like him, just before that plane took off, over the wire came a story in which I was referred to as a consummate liberal. And that did it. I decided to stay behind in New York State. (Laughter.)

And I must say this—although I was going to say nothing at

all, because I don't want to use the 25 minutes they gave me—there's a lot I do want to tell you. I did note with some interest that the two biggest laughs from this rather difficult looking groups were for the postmaster general and Dan Quayle. (Laughter.)

I am going to do something unusual now in this, what appears I think to be the last time I'll be able to speak as a public official, because nothing is going to happen over the next couple of weeks—and that didn't strike me until I sat down and started making some notes. But maybe especially because it is the last opportunity—there is a whole lot I want to get in. And because of that I'll stay close to my notes, closer than I usually do—and I'll rush a bit, if you don't mind, because I want you to have time to do the questions and answers. You know by now that I was elected a private citizen—(laughter)—effective January 1st.

It wasn't my first choice. Abraham Lincoln's familiar line in a similar situation, which I think the President used the other day, comes to mind. He said he felt like a young boy who has just stubbed his toe; it hurt too much to laugh, but he was too old to cry. The temptation, you should know, is to whine, you know—(laughter)—at least a bit—Why not?—you served 12 years, you're entitled. And I caught myself doing that.

I began pointing out to people that even since the Republican landslide on November 8th, it's been getting dark outside a little earlier every day. (Laughter.) You notice that? (Laughter. Applause.) The whining is not what we need. So let me talk to you about some of the things I learned on the way back to private life, and there's a lot. Let's talk just a bit about America and how together we can make her stronger and sweeter. Founded by the most optimistic people in history, in just 200 years, as we all know, would become the most dominant military and economic machine, and the greatest engine of opportunity that the world has ever seen.

But recently, say, within the last 15 years, we have made some terrible mistakes as well. We produced two devastating recessions that stripped from millions of our middle-class families the basic promise of the American dream, and even the simple security of steady work; mistakes that for millions more have produced lives of sheer desperation, dependence, and despair.

Government did not create all these all these problems, but government didn't solve them either. And the people know that. Many of them are frightened, resentful, even angry. The conservative Republicans measured that seething unhappiness with polls, then designed some painless home remedies which they strung together in a new political agenda that they call now the "Contract With America." And tell us it will solve our problems. I don't think so.

Some of the agenda puts the spotlight on relevant issues—at least for the moment. But the truth is, the contract fails to deal substantially with the fundamental problems we face. It's not a plan—it's an echo of selected polls. It adds nothing to the opinion surveys. It makes absolutely no demand on our political leadership, other than that they set sail in whatever direction the political winds appear to be blowing at the moment.

It offers a kind of plastic populism, epitomized by its bold promise of a balanced budget that will bend—or probably break—when tested with the full weight of our real problems. We need something much sturdier. We need an agenda that deals with our real problems—all of them, especially the toughest ones—and proposes real, concrete solutions, even if they are politically inconvenient. The truth is—and I think we all know this, too: America is faced with a double-barreled challenge to our future. The most significant is an economy that is rewarding investors for sure, but at the same time threatening our workers.

You tell a $30,000-a-year factory worker in Georgia or California that this is a growing economy, this third-wave economy, and see what reaction you get. The second challenge is the frightening cultural corruption of drugs, degradation, violence, and children having children, that's deteriorating our cities, crippling much of our potential work force, and alienating many of us from one another. And it is cultural. It is a cultural problem.

But the conservative Republican contract deals only superficially with our economic challenge, and offers us little more than castigation and negativism with respect to our cultural weakness.

Now, Democrats should show America that we can do better. We should start by reaffirming our fundamental democratic principles, beginning with the confidence that this country can provide opportunity for everyone willing to earn it. And the first mistake would be to give up on that aspiration, to believe that somehow we are not as strong as we thought we were—we can't do it—take up the gangplank!—we can't afford them: That would be a mistake, an excuse if not a mistake, a cynical excuse for not making the tough decisions that will make it possible for us to realize what is obvious, enormous potential strength still unused.

Our strong suit as Democrats has always been our concern for the vast majority of Americans who must work for a living—that's where we come from. That means we are committed to creating good jobs in a strong free-enterprise system, and to making sure that every working family in this country can earn enough to live with a reasonable degree of security and comfort. We believe that as part of the Democratic bargain every American has responsibilities.

Everyone who can work should work, instead of expecting others to pay their way. Businesses that thrive should share the rewards with their workers fairly—business has a responsibility as well. And government should help create jobs, not discourage them; nor should it burden the rewards of work with unreasonable heavy taxes.

Now, we believe in law and order. I have built more prison cells than all of the governors in history of New York State before me put together. But we will insist on fairness, and privacy, and civil rights. We agree with Lincoln that we should have only the government we need. But we agree with Lincoln, as well, that we must have all the government we need. We must have all the government we need.

And so a balanced budget that fails to meet the basic needs of the struggling middle class or the desperate poor would be an emblem of failure. We believe in the common sense value of sticks, but we also believe in the common sense power of carrots. We believe that prevention is always a good idea, and almost always cheaper.

We'd rather preserve a family than build an orphanage. We believe that we're too good as a people to seek solutions by hurting the weakest among us—especially our children. And at our wisest—at our wisest, and it's not always true. It is probably not true at this moment. But at our wisest, we believe that we are all in this together, that Jeremiah was right, thousands of years ago, that we will find our own good in the good of the whole community.

Now, this is not the time or the place to give all the details of what we can and must do to deal with the challenges and opportunities, while living up to these principles. But we should reflect on enough of them, and I have the responsibility to give you at least enough of them so that you can see that the agenda offered by the Contract is obviously incomplete, and utterly inadequate to this moment in American history. Most of all, we need to generate more jobs.

We'll accept that—jobs that pay a living wage and make hope a possibility, and a global economy, where labor often costs less in other places in the world—and that's the key. This is a complex challenge. But the Republicans would have us believe that the solution is remarkably simple.

Now, do you know how hard it is? Taiwan and that part of the world, in China, Mexico—they can make things a lot cheaper than you can. That puts an enormous pressure on your manufacturing. How do the Republicans deal with this problem? That's why the $30,000-a-year factory worker is scared to death. He knows it. He knows the investors are getting richer, and everybody is downsizing here, and the competition is enormous all over the world—a competition that I grew up without having to face.

Well, their proposal—the Republican proposal is right out of the permanent conservative Republican playbook. Cut the tax on capital gains, boost the defense budget, amend the Constitution to enforce a balanced budget. But let's not get bogged down in the awkward details about what we'd actually have to cut. Cut the taxes, boost the defense budget, and then provide a balanced budget. Does it sound familiar to you? Do you remember hearing that before? Cut your income, raise your expenses, and promise the bank that, this time, you're sure you can make ends meet. Does it sound familiar? It's nothing more than deja voodoo. (Laughter.)

In the early '80s—in the early '80s, the conservative Republicans promised huge tax cuts, a huge military, and a balanced budget—and we wound up, as we all know, with a deep recession and $4 trillion more in debt. Now, why is it different now? Why would it work any differently now? Has something changed? Has there been some kind of cosmic alteration? Only the language has changed.

In the '80s, they talked about the magic of supply side. Now, they have thought up a new way to count. It's called dynamic scoring. Do you know what dynamic scoring means? It means that, for every basket they put in the whole, they get ten points. That's dynamic scoring. And it would be wonderful if it were as easy as that—free up the wealth in the hands of the wealthy, and it will eventually take care of all of us. Now, this country tries that every so often. We tried it in the '80s—the early '80s.

But then the truth re-emerges. Life is more complicated and harder. It includes bothersome details, like a national deficit, leashed in by President Clinton, but ready to run wild at the least relaxation or provocation. Life includes popular entitlement programs that won't be around for our children at all, if we cannot bring ourselves to make intelligent, but different sacrifices now. Everybody in this room knows it. In every conversation in Washington or New York or the capitals of the country, where people know what they're talking about, they all say the same thing. "You must do something about Social Security." We all know that. "You must deal with Medicare." You can't deal with our deficit problem without doing something about Social Security and Medicare.

However, it's political poison, so we won't do it. But didn't you just tell me that, if we don't do something about it, we're in terrible trouble? Yes. And then you tell me that it's going to be very difficult to deal with it politically. Yes. And what do you prescribe then? Keep yourself alive politically, and let the country die. Am I exaggerating? Do you hear it differently? You write about it. You write about it glibly. Everybody comments on it—most of the time, snidely. But nobody changes it. Warren Rudman leaves. Paul Tsongas creates a group. Peter Peterson writes books.

Everybody is saying the same thing, and all the people who are bright, saying they're right, and admitting—at the same time—we do not have the will to change it. Why don't you at least say this to the American people. Why don't you say, "Look, let's get this clear, because I have the obligation to tell the truth." Who knows? Maybe there is a heaven. Worse than that, maybe there's a hell. (Laughter.)

Maybe I'm going to be accountable. Maybe I'd better tell you the truth. So, I'm going to take a chance.

Ladies and gentlemen, all the tax cuts in the world won't wave you. They're popular, but we need a double bypass—and we're talking about giving you cosmetic surgery. And the reason we're doing that is, it's too tough to give you a bypass. We have to cut with a knife. That's very expensive. It's very costly. It's unpleasant for you. We have to do Social Security. We have to do Medicare. You have to apply a needs test of some kind. Everybody knows it.

Now, why, therefore, don't the Republicans tell you that? Well, because they're into popularity. Why don't we tell you that? Because we're into popularity, too. (Laughter.) But we're going to say this to you. As long as the Republicans are in power in the Congress, and as long as it's absolutely clear that they will have a

Pavlovian response to whatever you tell them in the polls, start telling them in the polls that you've finally awakened. You know they have to do something about Social Security and Medicare. Please do Social Security and Medicare. They will write a new Contract with America, addendum to the Contract with America. We've seen the latest poll. It just came in over the Internet. Okay. You can have Social Security. (Laughter/Applause.)

There's another—there is another inconvenient truth, and that is that you have to make investments if you want to get returns. The Republicans especially should know that. And that means, if we want to be the high tech capital of the world—which you have to be, because if you're going to compete with cheap labor, how are you going to do it? You're going to have to make things with exquisite high tech capacity and superb productivity so that you can make things better and faster and different from the things that they can make—even with cheaper labor.

How else do you do it? The only other way is to expand a whole other thing beyond manufacturing, make exquisite improvements in services. We're doing that. We're the service capital of the world already—and we will stay that way for a long time, especially as long as New York stays strong, because you have banking, investment banking, and a lot of that there, publishing, et cetera. We're doing fine with services. On the manufacturing side, you can't do it without high tech. You have to do what we're doing in New York State—make a unique lens that we just sold to the Japanese. And when I complained to the University of Rochester about selling a unique lens to the Japanese, who are so good at replicating our products and getting—and producing something cheaper, they said, "Don't worry about it. We're working on a second lens." (Laughter.)

Making a new mammography machine on Long Island through high tech—a mammography machine that solves the problem that the woman has with the old machine, where she has to press herself up against this plate, where there's constriction, discomfort, and a poor picture. This one inclines. Bennett X-ray. You incline and gravity does the work. And there's a full picture. And my daughter, the radiologist loves it. And the woman is pleased by it. And the physician who has to operate feels better about it because he has a better picture. And we sell it to the Germans that make surgical instruments. And when I say to Bennett X-ray, "I created a center of high technology. Now you take this wonderful product. You send it to the Germans. How long before they replicate it?" He says, "Five months." I said, "Well, what are we going to do about that?" He said, "Don't worry about it, Governor. We're working on digitalizing it. We're taking the digital engineers from Grumman who have gone down, because they're no longer making planes. They're coming here. They're working on our mammography machine." You have to stay one step ahead of them in high tech.

That's the way you became great the first time around. You used to make all the things of value in this world. You were the makers and the sellers, the creditors and the bankers. That's how we became dominant. You can't get out of that business now because you're in a global economy. You have to make things. That means high tech. That means research. That means investment, investment, investment. And someone has to pay for it. There are plenty of good way of making our workers better equipped, too. And you can't do that.

You can't leave that factory worker where he is now, or she is now, at $30,000, and say, "Look, in this high tech world where we have to be smarter and slicker than they are, I'm afraid you're going to fall behind because you don't have the training." The GI Bill is a good idea for workers. Training vouchers is a good idea. Head Start is absolutely essential—learning technologies.

Is there any way you can explain how every kid in the United States of America doesn't have the opportunity to learn at a computer? How do you explain that to yourself? The richest place in world history, with all the tremendous wealth you have. How do you explain to yourself that there are kids who never see a computer—in my state, where people have Porsches parked or BMWs parked next to Jaguars? How do you explain it, when you're selling the airwaves for billions of dollars that you didn't even expect to have? Vice President Al Gore is right. Let's take some of that money and invest it in learning technologies.

Tax cut—hell of an idea. Learning technologies—an even better idea. Make your children the smartest in the world. Everybody knows that that's the avenue to the future. You write tracts about it. Kids write essays about it in the 8th grade.

But we're not doing it. That's the real world. It means investing, then capitalize, on the most extensive higher education system in the world. Promoting its strength and research, and making sure that it does not—that it becomes accessible to everybody. It means infrastructure. There is no money for infrastructure. Have you heard any Republican step forward and say, "And another thing we're going to do is we're going to build the infra-structure." Why? Infrastructure is an arcane word. You get no political points for infrastructure.

I wish I could think of some sexy way to say roads, bridges, telecommunication, fiber optics. Infrastructure. Forty percent of the roads and bridges are in trouble. Overseas, they spent $6 billion, Maglev, they're way ahead of you. You cannot succeed economically unless you invest in infrastructure. Where are you going to get the money? They didn't even mention it. How could you not mention it? Is there anybody alive with any brains at all who knows anything about the economy who would not say to you that, "Of course, we must invest more in the infrastructure." Or do they get challenged?

Does the public rise up after they have heard somebody on television say, "Well, I'll never vote for you. You never even men-tioned—what was that—infrastructure." Infrastructure. (Laugh-ter.)

Those conservative Republicans cannot deny that all of these investments are essential. They simply ignore them because they're politically difficult truths, and because the polls don't give you points for arcane things like infrastructure. They know America needs a double bypass. And they know they're only sug-gesting cosmetic surgery. But as long as its popular, that's what they're going to give you.

Now, massive tax cuts of any kind would surely ring the popu-larity bell. But would you insist on them, if it meant that local tax rates would explode across the country—which they could, if you cut back programs that the states are going to have to pay for instead. Would they insist on tax cuts if they knew that bridges would collapse, that the deficit might go up again, that you were failing to meet your educational needs? And if we can afford to lower taxes, would you give 70 percent of the immediate benefits to people who make $100,000 a year, or would you give 70 per-cent of the immediate benefits to the ordinary families across America?

And as long as you Republicans are so quick to point out that the people have spoken—who told you? The poll. Why don't you take a poll on it. Mr. and Mrs. America, we're going to give you a tax cut. What do you want? A tax cut the immediate benefit of which goes to—70 percent of which goes to the people above 100,000, or one that goes to people under 100,000? What do you think the poll would say? How about this one. Mr. and Mrs. America, would you like to shorten the congressional session and cut everybody's salary in half—senators and congressmen? What do you think they'd say? (Laughter.)

Last time I looked, it was 82 percent said yes. I didn't see a single Republican hold up, "The people have spoken." (Laughter.)

Of course, Democrats respect and believe in the efficiency of capitalism. A capital gains tax cut, in some circumstances, could be a very, very good thing. Deregulation—a very, very good thing. I did a lot of it in my own state. But if our system works only for investors and leaves millions of our people without the skills or opportunity to do more than tread water against the tide, our system fails. Now, if they're silent on these important things, what are they loudest on? Now, I'm really going to have to rush—and it's a shame.

Welfare. Why? Because it's popular. Don't you see what's happened? They've turned the middle class against the crowd beneath them. In the depression, you know, when everybody was angry, in 1932, whom did they blame? They blamed the power. The people who made it happen.

The bankers. The government. Everybody turned on the government—and they were right. And what's happened this time? Now they've turned the middle class downward. Instead of looking up at the people with the wealth, they're looking down at the people who are the victims. And who are you blaming?

The immigrants. That's easy. They have no political power, really, to speak of. Forget the fact that everybody here is an immigrant and that we all started by killing the only real entitled people to the place—the Native Americans. We butchered them. We savaged them. Everybody else is an intruder by your popular current definition. Forget that, because I'm lucky to be here now. It's the immigrants who are our problem. It's that baby who's making a baby. Forget about the fact that you allowed her, at the age of two, to be a toddler in streets surrounded by pimps and prostitutes and every kind of disorientation, that you allowed her to be seduced by somebody with a crack pipe when she was only nine years old.

Forget about that, that you allowed that society, that you allowed it to happen. She's the problem. Punish her. Punish the mother. No benefits for that child. Stick the child in an orphanage. You really think that's the answer? I don't.

In New York State we have problems, but we have answers, too, and they're not orphanages. We can show you ways to bring down teenage pregnancy dramatically, and we have with the new Avenues to Dignity program in New York. That's not as popular as draconian devices, like what they want to do with welfare or the death penalty. In the end, behind nearly every one of the Republican proposals lurks the same harshness and negativity. And I think we need better from our leaders than to have them distill our worst instincts and then bottle the bitter juices and offer them back to us as a magic elixir.

We need a cure, not a reaffirmation of our distress. We must understand that our great social problems are not visited upon us like earthquakes and floods. They are uniformly avoidable disasters. And with intelligent and timely action, we can prevent them before they pull our children down. Punishment has its place, of course. But prevention requires more than fear. In New York, the movement toward prevention is the strongest element in our approach to health care.

Incidentally, that's what reforming health care should be all about, prevention. The reason you need to cover those 39 million people is not compassion. It's not that they're not getting health care. They are getting health care. In my state, everybody gets health care, even the people without insurance. They fall down in the street and they're taken to the emergency room. Or they come with a terrible pain in their belly that would have been nothing if they had been insured and been to a doctor early, but now is acute. And we take care of them. What would we do, let them die? "You have no Medicaid. You have no insurance. Lay here and die." Of course not. We operate. You can find in the hospitals of New York City women and men on machines being kept alive for nobody knows how long except God, without any insurance, without any name, and we take care of them. You can't afford that.

Health care costs are going through the roof everywhere except in New York State. And they're high there, but we're the lowest-growing in the United States of America. That surprises a lot of people.

You have to do something about those 39 million people. And if Congress closed its eyes because it couldn't find a proper solution last time, you can't simply say, "This is too difficult; leave the problem there." You will go bankrupt. Really? Of course. You all know that. It's not just Ira Magaziner. You can't make it go away by saying, "Well, it was very unpopular." So do something else. Do something like what we're doing in New York. At least let the children of working people get insurance, get them into plans. We subsidize them to get them into plans. Why? Prevention. If you can vaccinate them, it's cheaper than trying to deal with their disease; so, too, with drugs. What is the answer to drugs? Look, you can build all the prisons you want.

You can contrive all the draconian punishments you want. You can say what the Republicans say, that more police, more prisons, more executions and reversing the ban on assault weapons will take care of the drugs and take care of the crime. It won't. Forget all about the complicated talk. Imagine this. Imagine a village. Imagine a village where the young people are drinking at a poisoned lake. And it makes them mad, and they come in every night to the village and they commit mayhem. And they rape and they kill and you arrest more and more of them and you stick them into jails in the village, and the jails are getting bigger and bigger and you have more and more village police and the villagers are complaining because they can't afford it.

And the generation of criminals keeps pouring out of the hills, having come from the poison lake. Wouldn't somebody with some brains say, "For God's sakes, let's dry up the lake; let's find another source of water"? Of course you would. But why aren't you doing it here? Why doesn't it occur to you that unless you stop the generation of these drug-ridden people who become criminals and then violent criminals—your biggest problem now in terms of crime: children with guns. You're not going to get at that. Take it from me.

I told you, I've built more prison cells than all the governors in history before me put together, and it's not going to work. Ask any policeman. Fifteen years ago they would have told you something else. You have cultural problems. I'm going to have to end it now, and it really is a shame because I'm leaving out a lot of the good stuff. (Laughter.)

I really am. But let me leave with maybe the largest point, and maybe the largest point that I have learned in public life, and it's something that I kind of intuited before I was in public life. It's something I spoke about in my first speech before I ever even ran, and this was up in Buffalo in 1973 and I was talking about mama and papa and what was important about mama and papa and what they taught me, these two illiterate people, what they taught me by their example.

And what they taught me, basically—and then a Vincencian priest, you know, added to it, and then good books, you know, taught you most of all, that you're going to spend your whole life learning things and experiencing things, most of all disappointment and occasionally moments of joy. But in the end, you've got to find some raison d'etre. You have to find some reason for living. You have to find something to believe in. And for it to work, it has to be larger than you, that you will discover that you are not enough to satisfy yourself. Now, you might get to be 70 years old before you figure it out, but sooner or later you'll figure it out, that you must have something larger than yourself to hold on to.

Where have you gone, Joe DiMaggio, Bobby Kennedy, Martin Luther King, Jr.; some great cause, some great purpose? The Second World War did that. I remember a little bit of that. The Second World War was a horrid thing, but it unified everybody in America. They were evil; we were good. They were Satan; we were doing God's work. And everybody got together—the men, the women, the blacks, everybody; forget about poor, forget about middle class; forget about everything else.

There's a grander purpose here. There's a greater truth here, something we can give ourselves to, and we'll fight like hell. And we did. We haven't had anything like that since, and you don't have it now.

You're turning those white factory workers all over the country against people of color. You're turning them against the immigrants. They're blaming them. And I understand why they're blaming them. Their life is vulnerable. They say, "You're doing nothing for me, everything for them." That's the truth of it. You know it. We all talk about it. We don't all write about it that clearly, but you know that the society is being fragmented.

It used to be the middle class against the rich, but now somehow, I think with a little encouragement from some of the politicians, you have turned the middle class to look downward instead of up. And they're now pitted against the poorest. So here are the least powerful people in your society, the least fortunate, squabbling with one another.

Ladies and gentlemen, unless we find a way to put this whole place together, unless we find a way to see that your interest depends upon your seeing the child in South Jamaica, that Latina, that little Hispanic girl who just had a baby, that little black girl who just had a baby, as your child, or unless you see that factory worker in Georgia as your father about to lose his job, unless you understand that it's not as a matter of love, not even at Christmas and Hanukkah time; I wouldn't ask that of anybody in a political context. It's too much to use the word compassion. Forget that. You'll lose.

As a matter of common sense, you cannot afford the loss of

productivity. You cannot afford the cost of drug addiction. You cannot afford it. We will not make it in this country unless we invest in dealing with those problems. And to deal with those problems, you have to give them other avenues to dignity instead of streets of despair. You will not frighten them into being good. You will not punish them into stopping drugs. You have to teach them. How to teach them?

Have a crusade; not just a rhetorical crusade, a real crusade. Invest in it. How would you teach children not to have sex too soon, to treat it as a great gift, not to be violent, not to take the drugs? How would you teach them? How do you teach anybody? Well, at home; their family is broken. In school; the teacher is too busy. In the church, the temple, the mosque; if they went there, it wouldn't be a problem. How do you teach them? Let the government teach them with laws. There's a role there, yes.

What's the best teaching instrument you have? Television. Yes, that's right. Why don't we teach them every night on prime time? Well, we have Partnership for a Drug-Free America. Once every week or two weeks they'll see those great commercials by the Partnership for a Drug-Free America. You read the New York Times this week. Drug use is up with teenagers. Why? Part of the reason, Partnership for a Drug-Free America isn't being seen enough. How do you explain that to yourself? You know it works.

You know the best thing you can do is teach the children not to take the drugs. The best way to teach them is television. Why aren't you on prime time? How can you settle for once a week or once every two weeks? If you were a mother of a child in South Jamaica, my neighborhood, and you knew that they were out there, going to tempt her with a crack pipe, and you had to go to work, would you settle for a stick-it note on the refrigerator once a week saying, "Hey, dear, if they come at you with a pipe, make sure you don't take it. See you tonight. Mother." Would you settle for that?

We're settling for it as a society. You want to talk about tax cuts? You want to talk about all these nice things? Talk about the real problems. Talk about how to invest in your economy, how to create jobs, how to invest in a real crusade that would have to—put up some money. Buy some time. Sit down with Tisch at NBC and all the others. Say, "We'll put up 5 million bucks. We want you to do the same." Let's saturate the place. Let's have billboards. Let the National Press Club write about it. Let all the community groups talk about it. Let's go at this problem for real because it's killing them and it's killing us.

Look, I lost an election. I've lost more than one, but I've learned a whole lot on the way, and I haven't forgotten any of it. And I'm telling you that I am absolutely certain we are not being honest about our problems. And the person who stands up and is honest with America and reminds America that they're now in charge—politicians used to think of themselves as shepherds. That's all over now.

Now the politicians are following the sheep. Read the polls. They'll tell you where they should go to pasture. And as long as you know that, you had better send the right signals to your government, because if you tell them you want the death penalty, you'll get it. If you tell them you want tax cuts, you'll get it. If you tell them to take up the gangplank, you'll get it. If you tell them to ignore sick people, you'll get it. If you tell them to ignore the poor, you'll get it. If you tell them to victimize young children, you'll get it.

Be careful what you ask for, because they're listening for you. And ask for the right things. Ask for the truth. Ask for the real solutions to the real problems. I learned that. I won't forget it. Thank you for your patience.

---

## CONGRESSIONAL TERM LIMITS[1]
### HENRY J. HYDE[2]

---

In 1994–1995, a highly publicized and controversial issue was a proposed constitutional amendment limiting the length of terms that could be served by members of the U.S. Congress. Voter dissatisfaction with political leadership had led to the passage of such laws on a local level in some communities and states.

Many people believed that the country's elected officials had become slaves to opinion polls and that incumbents had an unfair advantage over their challengers in most elections. In this view, the country was "afflicted with a class of parasites—career politicians—who devote their lives to perpetuating themselves in office by spending the people's money." (Hendrik Hertzberg, *The New Yorker*, March 17, 1995, p. 2)

[1]Delivered in the United States House of Representatives, Washington, D.C. on March 29, 1995.

[2]For biographical note see Appendix.

These sentiments led to the introduction in the House of Representatives of four separate constitutional amendments to limit the number of terms which senators and representatives could serve. All of the bills eventually failed, but the debate in the House attracted national attention. *The Congressional Record* reports that forty-two members of the House delivered speeches on the issue. While it would be difficult to determine which of those speeches were the most effective or influential, one address received more attention than the others. This was the address by Representative Henry J. Hyde, Republican of Illinois, who opposed term limitations. "America needs leaders, it needs statesmen and it needs giants—and you don't get them out of the phone book," Hyde told the House. "This corrosive attack on the consent of the governed stems from two sources—one is well meaning but misguided and the other are those who really in their hearts hate politics and despise politicians. . .The case for term limits is a rejection of professionalism in politics." (*New York Times,* March 30, 1995, p. A9)

*Representative Hyde's speech:* Mr. Chairman, I ask that no member ask me to yield until I finish because I do not want to be interrupted.

I want to tell you how unpleasant it is to take the well in militant opposition to something that is so near and dear to the hearts of so many of my colleagues and members whom I revere, but I just cannot be an accessory to the dumbing down of democracy. And I think that is what this is. I might also say, parenthetically, that it is a little amusing to see the stickers that have been worn by so many of my colleagues. It says, "term limits, yes." It does not say, "term limits now." It says, "term limits, yes."

I am reminded of the famous prayer of Saint Augustine who said, Dear God, make me pure, but not now.

If someone told you on election day you had to vote for a particular person, you would wonder if you were back in the Soviet Union. What is the essential differences if they tell you you may not vote for this person? They have limited your range of choices. You have narrowed the circle of possibilities. You have denied a fundamental right free people have in a free country. If this were a trial, I would call as my first witnesses the Founding Fathers who directly rejected term limits.

Chief Justice Earl Warren, in the famous case of Powell versus MacCormick, 1969, said, and I quote, "a fundamental principle of our representative democracy is, in Hamilton's words, 'that the people should choose whom they please to govern them.' As Madison pointed out at the convention," still quoting Justice Warren, "this principle is undermined as much by limiting whom the people can select as by limiting the franchise itself."

In 1788, in New York, in debating ratifying the Constitution, Robert Livingston asked a haunting question: "Shall we then drive experience into obscurity?" He called that an absolute abridgment of the people's rights.

George Orwell, in a review of a book by Bertrand Russell, said it has become the task of the intellectual to defend the obvious. I make no pretense at being an intellectual, but defending experience against ignorance is certainly obvious.

Have you ever been in a storm at sea? I have, and I knew real terror until I looked up on the bridge and the old Norwegian skipper, who had been to sea for 45 years, was up there sucking on his pipe. And I can tell you that was reassuring.

When that dentist bends over with the drill whirring, do you not hope he has done that work for a few years?

And when the neurosurgeon has shaved your head and they have made the pencil mark on your skull where they are going to have the incision and he approaches with the electric saw, ask him one question, are you a careerist?

Is running a modern complex society of 250 million people and a $6 trillion economy all that easy? To do your job, to have a smattering of ignorance, in Oscar Levant's phrase, you have to know something about the environment, health care, banking and finance and tax policy, farm problems, weapons systems, Bosnia and Herzegovina and North Korea, not to mention Nagorno-Karabakh, foreign policy, the administration of justice, crime and punishment, education and welfare, budgeting in the trillions of dollars and immigration. And I have not scratched the surface.

We need our best people to deal with these issues. We in Congress deal with ultimate issues: life and death, war and peace, drawing the line between liberty and order. And do you ever really doubt that America will never again have a real crisis? With a revolving-door Congress, where will we get our Everett Dirksens, our Scoop Jackson, our Arthur Vandenbergs, our Hubert Humphreys, our Barry Goldwaters, our Sam Ervins? You do not get them out of the phone book. Where did Shimon Peres and Yitzak Rabin get the self-confidence to negotiate peace for their people with the PLO? I will tell you where: experience, bloody, bloody experience.

To those of you that are overwhelmed by the notion that this is a very popular cause, let me remind you of what Edmund

Burke told the electors of Bristol, November 3, 1774. He said, a member of Parliament owes to his constituency his highest fidelity. But he also owes them his best judgment and he does not owe his conscience to anybody.

I once told an incoming class of freshmen back when they let me speak to them at lunch that they have to know the issues to be prepared to lose their seat over or they would do real damage here. To me, this is such an issue.

The unstated premise of term limits is that we are progressively corrupted the longer we stay around here. In answer to that I say, look around. You will see some of the finest men and women you will ever encounter in your life. The 12 apostles had their Judas Iscariot. We have a higher ratio than that. And I will tell you, I will not surrender. I will not concede to the angry, pessimistic populism that drives this movement, because it is just dead wrong.

Our negative campaigning, our mud-slinging, our name calling has made anger the national recreation. But that is our fault, not the system's. America needs leaders. It needs statesmen. It needs giants, and you do not get them out of the phone book.

News is always better? What in the world is conservative about that? Have we nothing to learn from the past, tradition, history, institutional memory? Do they not count?

They have a saying in the provinces, Ignorance is salvageable, but stupid is forever.

This is not conservative. It is radical distrust of democracy. It is cynical. It is pessimistic, devoid of the hope and the optimism that built this country.

This corrosive attack on the consent of the governed stems from two sources. One is well meaning but misguided, and the other are those who really in their heart hate politics and despise politicians.

I confess, I love politics and I love politicians. They invest the one commodity that can never be replaced, their time, their family life, their privacy, and their reputation. And for what? To make this a better country.

Oh, incumbents have an advantage. I guess they do, although not necessarily. You have a record to defend. You have voted on hundreds of bills. And you get socked with them by your challenger who has nothing to defend, and you better be ready to explain how you voted back in 1988 on Gramm-Rudman or something like that.

But listen to me, it is 11:30 at night. And it is January and the snow is whirling outside the window. And I am in a banquet hall. I am at my one-millionth banquet. I am sitting there as we are honoring the mayor of one of my local towns, and they have not even introduced the commissioner of streets yet. And I am exhausted. And I look out the window at the snowstorm and I wonder where my opponent is.

He does not even know he is my opponent. He is home, stroking his collie dog, smoking a Macanudo, sipping from a snifter of Courvoisier and watching an R-rated movie on cable. But I am at that banquet.

Again and again, I will tell you why you have a leg up, good constituent service, accessibility, and availability. You ought to have a leg up. You have made an investment challengers never make. I will not apologize for that.

The case for term limits is a rejection of professionalism in politics. Career politician is an epithet. Careerism, they say, places too much focus on getting reelected and not on the public interest. That is a perfect nonsequitur. You get reelected by serving the public interest. Professionals, my friends, will run this government. Only they will not be elected, they will be the faceless, nameless, try-to-get-them-on-the-phone, unaccountable permanent bureaucracy.

There are two contradictory arguments which support this term-limits issue. One is that we are too focused on reelection, not close enough to the people. Then you have the George Will theory that we are too close to the people, too responsive, and we need a constitutional distance from them.

I suggest any cause that is supported by two contradictory theories like this is standing on two stools which, as they separate, will give you an awful hernia.

Term limits limit the field of potential candidates. What successful person in midlife will leave a career at 50 and try and pick up the pieces at 56 or 62? This job will become a sabbatical for the well-to-do elite and bored retirees. And if you listen carefully, if this ever becomes law, that shuffling sound you hear is the musical chairs being played in every legislature in the country. So the question of 1788 recurs. Shall we then drive experience into obscurity? Shall we perpetrate this absolute abridgment of the people's rights?

Listen, last June 6, I had the honor of standing on the beaches at Normandy with Bob Dole, Bob Michel, Sonny Montgomery,

Sam Gibbons, and John Dingell. I guess you would call us old bulls today. But we were very young when we fought in battle 50 years ago. I guess we were citizen soldiers and citizen sailors back then. By some perverse logic, you withhold from us the title of citizen legislators today.

But I heard the mournful, piercing sound of bag pipes from a British band, scattered among the sea of white crosses and the Stars of David, playing "Amazing Grace." And with eyes not quite dry, I read some of the names on the crosses until I came to one that had no name. It just had a cross, stating "Here Lies in Honored Glory a Comrade in Arms Known but to God."

Then I saw another and another like that. No name, no family, just heroism buried thousands of miles from home. It occurred to me what an unpayable debt we owe these people because they died for freedom, and a part of that freedom is to choose who will govern you.

I can never vote to disparage that freedom. I pray you cannot either.

I presume to speak for Sam Gibbons, Bob Stump, John Dingell, Sonny Montgomery, and yes, Bob Dole. Fifty years ago our country needed us and we came running. I think our country still needs us. Why do you want to stop us from running? Why do you want to drive experience into obscurity? Have you forgotten the report card we got last November?

I have one piece of advice: Trust the people.

# VIOLENCE AND TERRORISM

## FEAR AND TERROR[1]
### F. FORRESTER CHURCH IV[2]

Perhaps more than any other recent event, the bombing of the Federal Building in Oklahoma City on April 19, 1995, brought home to Americans the threat of terrorism in this country. Although angered by the bombing of the World Trade Center in New York City two years before and confused by the confrontations between the federal government agents and the Branch Davidians near Waco, Texas, the bombing of a government building in the middle of the country resulting in over a hundred deaths and injuries to many others shocked the public. That such an event could occur in the "heartland of America"—as almost every newspaper and television report described—convinced many Americans that terrorism was no longer an activity confined to the Middle East and Europe.

The immediate reaction was that the deed must have been committed by agents of a foreign government or a radical religious group whose popular stereotype Rev. F. Forrester Church described as "bearded, wiry, dark-eyed, alien, inscrutable, fanatical, terrifying."

The bombing, just after Easter, caused Dr. Church of the All Souls Unitarian Church in New York City, to abandon his planned sermon the following Sunday and to discuss his own reactions to the event and to warn against the dangers of stereotyping different cultural, religious, and ethnic groups. This was not the first time Dr. Church had preached on the subject of cultural and religious differences, intolerance, and terrorism. Nine years before—almost to the day, on April 20, 1986, Dr. Church had delivered a sermon on terrorism following the United States' bombing of five alleged "terrorist centers" in Libya, which resulted in the death of thirty-seven people and the injury

[1]Delivered to the congregation of All Souls Unitarian Church, New York City on April 23, 1995.
[2]For biographical note see Appendix.

of ninety-three others. (See *Representative American Speeches, 1986–1987* for the text of this speech.)

A distinctive feature of Dr. Church's sermons is his candor with the congregation concerning his own feelings, reactions, and even personal shortcomings. In delivering his sermons, Reverend Church seems to be sharing his thoughts, rather than preaching to his audience.

*Reverend Church's speech:* How very long ago Easter seems. Only a week ago we gathered in this peaceful sanctuary to trumpet the victory of love over death. One week later we are left to sort through the rubble and carnage that litter the once quiet streets of Oklahoma City, our hearts possessed with grief, anger, and fear. It's as if Easter this year has been turned on its head, the holy calendar reversed, resurrection first and then, three days later, the crucifixion.

Obviously whatever I had planned to speak about this morning is of no consequence in light of the week's events. In a single blast, the world we live in is unalterably changed.

There is little we can do about this. In fact, apart from the perilous, if completely understandable, urge for retribution, our grief, anger, and fear are accompanied by a hollow sense of powerlessness. I did send, on your behalf, the following overnight letter to our fellow Unitarian Universalists at the First Unitarian Church in Oklahoma City. It's only a gesture, but at times like this, watching at a distance, we are sometimes forced to rely on mere gestures. At least they connect us to those whose pain is more immediate than our own.

*Dear Unitarian Universalist Friends in Oklahoma City:*

*Please know how deeply we feel for you and your neighbors in the wake of the terrible tragedy that has befallen you, and indeed, our entire country. Having struggled with our own fears following the World Trade Center bombing two years ago, we in New York have at least a sense of the bewilderment you must surely be experiencing. Our prayers this Sunday are with you and the loved ones of those members of your congregation whose lives have been affected or swept away by this senseless, evil act. If we can be of any assistance whatsoever, please do not hesitate to call.*

*In faith and with profound sorrow,*

*Forrest Church (on behalf of the congregation of All Souls in New York City)*

First Unitarian Church is near the Federal Building in Oklahoma City. The impact of the bomb caused some structural damage. Two members of the church are among the missing, and therefore presumed dead. Carolyn and I will send a check directly to the church for their relief fund. I invite you to join us. Give it or send it to me and I'll pass it along. This too is a small thing, a gesture, but it connects us with our religious family. It permits us to do something, however small, at a time when so little we can say or do seems to matter all that much.

The question remains, how do we sort through the rubble and carnage? How can we extricate some meaning or guidance from this terrible tragedy? I am as off balance as you are. Having been transfixed by the television reports, I now want to run from them, from the images of horror, from the tears and the anger. I am looking for a good movie, even a bad movie, anything to take me away. And I will find one. I found one yesterday. I will find one today. But I also know that I must look deeper and further, both into myself and into the life we share as citizens of this country, even of the world.

I must look deeper into myself, in part because my initial response to the Oklahoma City bombing was to fix my attention and fear on a composite, stereotypical image of a Muslim terrorist: bearded, wiry, dark-eyed, alien, inscrutable, fanatical, terrifying. Even after I saw the composite drawings of the two suspects, I thought to myself, "Well, the one could be Arab. Perhaps the other is a bad rendering. After all, they caught that man on his way from Oklahoma City to Jordan, his bags filled with bomb-making material and photographs of American military sites."

His name was Amad Abrahim. They held him for sixteen hours. He was very cooperative. His bags were not filled with bomb-making material and photographs of American military sites. Nor did the other suspects I read about, Asad and Anis Siddiqy, have anything to do with the bombing. They were Queens taxi drivers working on an immigration problem. They lived with Mohammed Chaff. He too was grilled for fifteen hours. I understand that. All leads had to be scrupulously followed. But I also know that if I were given a multiple choice terrorist quiz two days ago, and asked to guess between Asad Siddiqy, Mohammed Chaff, Amad Abrahim, Timothy McVeigh, and Terry Nichols, I would have failed the test.

The threat of internationally sponsored murder and mayhem by such groups as the Hamas and Hesbollah is very real. An old friend of mine, Steve Emerson, author of the now-famous documentary "Jihad in America," presents the evidence in convincing detail. But I also know, or should know, that no people, no faith, have anything like a corner on hatred. Take the woman who said of our Muslim neighbors on a talk show this week, "No wonder this happened. These countries, their culture, have no respect for human life." Or the caller who threatened to blow up a discount variety store on Fifth Avenue owned by Syrian-born Albert Cabal. "We're going to get you and we're going to get your family." "This is not a question of anybody's country of origin," President Clinton reminds us. "This is not a question of anybody's religion. This was murder, this was evil, this was wrong. Human beings everywhere, all over the world, will condemn this out of their own religious convictions."

So I am troubled, deeply troubled, by my knee-jerk reaction. All of us are prejudiced. But when thoughtful people do not work hard to temper their prejudices, bigots—those who celebrate prejudice—will only be vested with more power. Bigots like Timothy McVeigh and Terry Nichols.

I've noticed that a favorite question posed by reporters to people on the street is some variation of, "Does it bother you that Americans are responsible for this?" "It devastates me," one woman replied. "I just can't believe that an American, that a human being, could do this." There are millions of Arab Americans, millions of Muslim Americans—Muslim American human beings. They are only as likely to buy the hatred spewed by the Hamas or Hesbollah as are white-bread Mid-Western Christian Americans likely to feed on the equally bigoted and dangerous paranoia fostered by groups like the Michigan Militia, led by Norman Olson, self-styled "pistol-packin' preacher," and gun store owner. Or the Arizona Patriots, whose members believe that the United States is being run by the Protocol of Zion or about to be conquered by the United Nations.

Friday's *New York Post* [Apr. 23, 1995] ran a cartoon of three Muslims laughing and burning an American flag at the base of the Statue of Liberty, which read "Give us your tired, your poor, your huddled masses, your terrorists, your murderers, your slime, your evil cowards, your religious fanatics, your welfare cheats." I can think of at least two flag-waving Christians wedded to their own perverse reading of the Bill of Rights, who would have laughed knowingly at that cartoon. Believing that our government has fallen prey to foreigners, welfare cheats, and slime, among whom they numbered Blacks and Jews, and obsessed with their guns, these two unimaginably sick Americans are responsible for the death of some two hundred innocent people, victims of the same kind of hate that such a cartoon unwittingly fosters.

Timothy McVeigh, a "quiet, shy church-going youth from upstate New York, who liked computers, basketball, and cars." Terry Nichols, a "good neighbor," with a bumper-sticker on his car that boasted the words, "American and Proud." The former, arrested carrying a licensed Glock semi-automatic pistol, loaded with hollow point bullets, known as cop-killers, slept with his guns. The latter was known to have experimented with making fertilizer bombs in his barn.

Tom Metzger, head of something called the White Aryan Resistance, said yesterday: "I have told people for years, at least since 1984, when The Order declared war on the central government of the United States that the government of this country—what we call the criminals—had better start listening to the dispossessed white people, the dispossessed majority. There was a hot war in the 1980's, and since then there's been a cold war, and now things are heating up again."

We don't need to look outside our borders or to another faith to discover our common enemy. He also lurks within, inspired not by the Koran but by the Book of Revelation, his hatred of the government fed by the incendiary, divisive anti-government rhetoric employed so successfully by certain of our political leaders, his fears fomented into paranoia and then violence by the American gun lobby.

We don't have to look any further than *The Turner Diaries*, a hateful, frightening book deemed the Bible of the survivalist movement. Positing the secret take-over of the government by Jews seeking to strip good Americans of their guns in an attempt to establish a new world order, the book begins with these words: "Today, it finally began. After all those years of talking—and nothing but talking—we have finally taken our first action. We are at war with the system, and it is no longer a war of words." Extremists blow up a federal office building at 9:15 in the morning. "Our worries about the relatively small size of the bomb were unfounded; the damage is immense. The scene in the courtyard was one of utter devastation. Overturned trucks and automobiles, smashed office furniture and building rubble were strewn wildly about—and so were the bodies of a shockingly large number of victims. They have clearly made the decision to portray the bombing of the FBI building as the atrocity of the century. All the bombings, arsons and assassinations carried out by the Left in this country have been rather small time in comparison."

And so we come to April 19th. The day that American patriots defended Lexington and Concord against the Redcoats in 1775. The day that survivalist Randy Weaver, holed up in Ruby Ridge, Idaho, was informed by compatriots of a government plot against him in 1992. The day that the Branch Davidians immolated themselves in 1993. And the day that white-supremacist, Richard Snell, who murdered a black police officer and a Jewish business man was to be executed in Arkansas in 1995. That was last Wednesday. With this date as a mantra, one right-wing newsletter, *The Montana Militia*, warned that Snell would die, "unless we act now!!!" Snell, a murderer, did die. So did 200 innocents. Two centuries after the first minutemen bravely fought at the Lexington bridge, two centuries after our founders, mindful of events leading up to the shot heard round the world, passed the second amendment to our nation's constitution establishing our right to a citizens' militia, a far deadlier blast in Oklahoma City has been heard round the world, and history itself, our own nation's history, lies twisted in the wreckage.

There will be great pressure in the days ahead to enact an Omnibus Counter-terrorism Act to protect us from Muslim fanatics. I wish only that certain of the most vociferous proponents of this legislation would examine their own consciences to ponder how their support for lifting a ban on semi-automatic weapons actually enhances the opportunity for terrorism to occur in this country. I hope they will hear their own words about protecting our sacred right to buy and keep arms echo back from the writings and voices of the hate mongers actually responsible for the tragedy in Oklahoma City. I hope they will think, at least a little, about how the seeds of division grow, how rhetoric that plays on our fears of one another, on our differences, the rhetoric that scapegoats, that pits neighbor against neighbor, can so easily blossom into full-blown bigotry, and with such devastating consequence.

One final thought. When we try to fight hatred with hate and fire with fire, we do not lessen but only compound the object of our enmity. We do not destroy the Randy Weavers of this world by sending federal agents to storm their Idaho shack, killing his wife and child in the crossfire. We do not extirpate the power expressed in David Koresh's paranoia and fascination with violence by killing four of his followers and then embargoing his compound until he and his sect immolate themselves. We do nothing to diminish the white-supremicism and anti-Semitism spewed by

Richard Snell when we execute him for his heinous crimes. As the tragedy in Oklahoma City reminds us, violence only begets more violence. Even the most just violence, whether institutional or accidental, only contributes to the climate of fear and hatred which spawns yet more violence in an endless spiral.

If we have learned anything, we should have learned this from the endless succession of terrorist activity in the Middle East. Now we can study it on our own soil. If I were asked yesterday whether the perpetrators of this unimaginably evil act should receive the death penalty, I would have said yes. Today, I say no. I couldn't bear for them to become martyrs for the next wave of Timothy McVeighs and Terry Nichols. Let the blood be on their hands, not ours.

I expect that we will execute them. When we do, even as I have wrestled this week with my own prejudice against Arab Americans, I will again, I am sure, wrestle against, and perhaps unsuccessfully, my own primitive, human desire for vengeance. Not my finest part, but part of me will cheer when these brutal men die. I am ashamed of that, but it is so.

What I will be far more ashamed of is this. I will be far more ashamed if I do not dedicate a greater part of my energy to combating—and that is not too strong a word—the climate of violence that is poisoning this country. Begin with guns. Ban more. Restrict others. Enforce and enhance licensing procedures. Make them difficult to buy. Enact severe penalties for illegal sale or possession. And drive every lackey of the American gun lobby from office, however high-minded and perversely patriotic his or her rhetoric.

I will also be ashamed if I do not do everything in my small power to reclaim the history and symbols of this great nation from the anti-American, anti-Christian white supremacist and survivalist zealots who have turned the courageous minutemen of Concord and the American Bill of Rights into fertilizer for their bombs. So far as it is in our power, and while admitting some necessary abridgment forced by prudence, we must not permit ourselves to be held hostage by our fears, driven to compromise precious American rights far more essential to the survival of this republic than the right to bear arms. The only way to do this is to answer fear, the fear these zealots and their unwitting political champions foment so successfully, with greater faith, the faith of our founders, a faith in one nation, indivisible, with liberty and justice for all. We must answer in the spirit of the people of

Oklahoma City, whose courage, bravery, self-sacrifice, and neighborly love remind us once again of what it really means to be a
true American. We must answer according to the best that is
within the human heart, not imitate the worst.

Perhaps the best way to counter fear with faith is to begin with
our own prejudices. These we can do something about, something more than a gesture. Tomorrow I shall call a Muslim cleric,
Shaykh Abd'Allah Ali, Leader of the Admiral Family Circle, and
invite him to preach at All Souls as soon as possible. This after-
noon, at the Adult Education Committee meeting, I will urge that
we devote a month next fall to the study of Islam. Most of us are
profoundly ignorant about the teachings of Islam, an ignorance
that feeds our prejudice.

In the meantime, mindful of life's fragility, let us remember
how fortunate we are. Please, treat one another with kindness. Be
thankful for the days we are given. There is time for us, there is
still time, time to love and also time to learn.

---

## VIOLENT CRIME: MYTHS, FACTS, AND SOLUTIONS[1]
### D. STANLEY EITZEN[2]

---

During the early 1990s violent crime was perceived by a large
number of Americans as the major problem facing the United
States. Surveys showed that most people regarded crime as the
most serious threat to their personal well-being and that of the
country. At all levels—local, state, and national—the common
response to the problem of crime was to enact more stringent laws
to punish the guilty in hope of deterring future criminal activity.
Little attention was given to understanding the causes.

Some law enforcement officials, criminologists, and scholars
spoke out against the prevailing belief that harsher penalties per
se would reduce violent crime. They sought to educate the public
about what they saw as the nature of crime and its causes. One

[1]Delivered at the 1995 Symposium "The Shadow of Violence: Unconsidered
Perspectives," at Hastings College in Hastings, Nebraska on March 13, 1995 at
10 a.m.
[2]For biographical note see Appendix.

such educational effort was a 1995 symposium held at Hastings College in Hastings, Nebraska, in March 1995. At the symposium, which was titled "The Shadow of Violence: Unconsidered Perspectives," participants explored a number of approaches to the problem that had not been widely considered.

One of the most important speeches at the meeting was the address by Dr. D. Stanley Eitzen, the John H. Sterm Distinguished Professor of the Department of Sociology at Colorado State University. Professor Eitzen stated his goal early in the speech, saying:

I am going to critique the prevailing thought about violent crime and its control because our perceptions about violent crime and much of what our government officials do about it is wrong.

Using statistics, surveys, government reports, research, and studies by experts, Eitzen sought to dispel myths about the public's perception of crime, to provide facts, and to suggest possible solutions. The speech was given to an audience of approximately one thousand students, faculty, and administrators in the Hastings College auditorium.

While the symposium received little coverage in the national media, Professor Eitzen's speech was brought to the public's attention when it was reprinted in *Vital Speeches of the Day.*

*Mr. Eitzen's speech:* My remarks are limited to violent street crimes (assault, robbery, rape, and murder). We should not forget that there are other types of violent crimes that are just as violent and actually greater in magnitude than street crimes: corporate, political, organized, and white collar. But that is another subject for another time. Our attention this morning is on violent street crime, which has made our cities unsafe and our citizens extremely fearful. What are the facts about violent crime and violent criminals and what do we, as a society, do about them?

I am going to critique the prevailing thought about violent crime and its control because our perceptions about violent crime and much of what our government officials do about it is wrong. My discipline—sociology—knows a lot about crime but what we know does not seem to affect public perceptions and public policies. Not all of the answers, however, are always crystal clear. There are disagreements among reasonable and thoughtful people, coming from different theoretical and ideological perspectives. You may, difficult as it seems to me, actually disagree with my analysis. That's all right. The key is for us to address this serious problem, determine the facts, engage in dialogue, and then work toward logical and just solutions.

What do criminologists know about violent crime? Much of what we know is counter intuitive; it flies in the face of the public's understanding. So, let me begin with some demythologizing.

*Myth 1: As a Christian nation with high moral principles, we rank relatively low in the amount of violent crime.* Compared with the other industrialized nations of the world, we rank number one in belief in God, "the importance of God in our lives," and church attendance. We also rank first in murder rates, robbery rates, and rape rates. Take homicide, for example: the U.S. rate of 10 per 100,000 is three times that of Finland, five times that of Canada, and nine times greater than found in Norway, the Netherlands, Germany, and Great Britain. In 1992, for example, Chicago, a city about one-fifth the population of the Netherlands had nine times more gun-related deaths than occurred in the Netherlands.

*Myth 2: We are in the midst of a crime wave.* When it comes to crime rates we are misled by our politicians, and the media. Government data indicate that between 1960 and 1970 crime rates doubled, then continued to climb through the 1970s. From 1970 to 1990 the rates remained about the same. The problem is with violent crime by youth, which has increased dramatically. Despite the rise in violent crime among youth, however, the *overall* violent crime rate actually has decreased in the 1990s.

Our perceptions are affected especially by the media. While crime rates have leveled and slightly declined during the 1990s, the media have given us a different picture. In 1993, for example, the three major networks doubled their crime stories and tripled their coverage of murders. This distortion of reality results, of course, in a general perception that we are in the midst of a crime wave.

*Myth 3: Serious violent crime is found throughout the age structure.* Crime is mainly a problem of male youths. Violent criminal behaviors peak at age 17 and by age 24 it is one-half the rate. Young males have always posed a special crime problem. There are some differences now, however. Most significant, young males and the gangs to which they often belong now have much greater firepower. Alienated and angry youth once used clubs, knives, brass knuckles, and fists but now they use Uzis, AK47s, and "street-sweepers." The result is that since 1985, the murder rate for 18-24 year-olds has risen 65 percent while the rate for 14-17 year-olds has increased 165 percent.

The frightening demographic fact is that between now and the year 2005, the number of teenagers in the U.S. will grow by 23 percent. During the next ten years, black teenagers will increase by 28 percent and the Hispanic teenage population will grow by about 50 percent. The obvious prediction is that violent crime will increase dramatically over this period.

*Myth 4: The most dangerous place in America is in the streets where strangers threaten, hit, stab, or shoot each other.* The streets in our urban places are dangerous, as rival gangs fight, and drive-by shootings occur. But, statistically, the most dangerous place is in your own home, or when you are with a boyfriend or girlfriend, family member, or acquaintance.

*Myth 5: Violent criminals are born with certain predispositions to- ward violence.* Criminals are not born with a criminal gene. If crime were just a function of biology, then we would expect crime rates to be more or less the same for all social categories, times, and places. In fact, violent crime rates vary considerably by social class, race, unemployment, poverty, geographical place, and other social variables. Research on these variables is the special contri- bution of sociology to the understanding of criminal behavior.

Let's elaborate on these social variables because these have so much to do with solutions. Here is what we know about these social variables:

1. The more people in poverty, the higher the rate of street crime.

2. The higher the unemployment rate in an area, the higher the crime rate. Sociologist William J. Wilson says that black and white youths at age 11 are equally likely to commit violent crimes but by their late 20s, blacks are four times more likely to be violent offenders. However, when blacks and whites in their late 20s are employed, they differ hardly at all in violent behavior.

3. The greater the racial segregation in an area, the higher the crime rate. Sociologist Doug Massey argues that urban poverty and urban crime are the consequences of extremely high levels of black residential segregation and racial discrimination. Massey says,

"Take a group of people, segregate them, cut off their capital and guess what? The neighborhoods go downhill. There's no other outcome possible."

As these neighborhoods go downhill and economic opportunities evaporate, crime rates go up.

4. The greater the family instability, the higher the probability

of crimes by juveniles. Research is sketchy, but it appears that the following conditions are related to delinquent behaviors: (a) intense parental conflict; (b) lack of parental supervision; (c) parental neglect and abuse; and (d) failure of parents to discipline their children.

5. The greater the inequality in a neighborhood, city, region, or society, the higher the crime rate. In other words, the greater the disparities between rich and poor, the greater the probability of crime. Of all the industrialized nations, the U.S. has the greatest degree of inequality. For example, one percent of Americans own 40 percent of all the wealth. At the other extreme, $14^{1}/_{2}$ percent of all Americans live below the poverty line and 5 percent of all Americans live below *one-half* of the poverty line.

When these social variables converge, they interact to increase crime rates. Thus, there is a relatively high probability of criminal behavior—violent criminal behavior—among young, black, impoverished males in inner cities where poverty, unemployment, and racial segregation are concentrated. There are about 5 million of these high-risk young men. In addition, we have other problem people. What do we do? How do we create a safer America?

To oversimplify a difficult and contentious debate, there are two answers—the conservative and progressive answers. The conservative answer has been to get tough with criminals. This involves mandatory sentences, longer sentences, putting more people in prison, and greater use of the death penalty. This strategy has accelerated with laws such as "three strikes and you're out (actually in)," and the passage of expensive prison building programs to house the new prisoners.

In my view, this approach is wrong-headed. Of course, some individuals must be put in prison to protect the members of society. Our policies, however, indiscriminately put too many people in prison at too high a cost. Here are some facts about prisons:

1. Our current incarceration rate is 455 per 100,000 (in 1971 it was 96 per 100,000). The rate in Japan and the Netherlands is one-tenth ours. Currently, there are 1.2 million Americans in prisons and jails (equivalent to the population of Philadelphia).

2. The cost is prohibitive, taking huge amounts of money that could be spent on other programs. It costs about $60,000 to build a prison cell and $20,000 to keep a prisoner for a year. Currently the overall cost of prisons and jails (federal, state, and local) is $29 billion annually. The willingness to spend for punishment reduces money that could be spent to alleviate other social prob-

lems. For example, eight years ago Texas spent 7 dollars on education for every dollar spent on prisons. Now the ratio is 4 to 1. Meanwhile, Texas ranks 37th among the states in per pupil spending.

3. As mentioned earlier, violent crimes tend to occur in the teenage years with a rapid drop off afterwards. Often, for example, imprisonment under "3 strikes and you're out" laws gives life imprisonment to many who are in the twilight of their criminal careers. We, and they, would be better off if we found alternatives to prison for them.

4. Prisons do not rehabilitate. Actually, prisons have the opposite effect. The prison experience tends to increase the likelihood of further criminal behavior. Prisons are overcrowded, mean, gloomy, brutal places that change people, but usually for the worse, not the better. Moreover, prisoners usually believe that their confinement is unjust because of the bias in the criminal justice system toward the poor and racial minorities. Finally, prisoners do not ever pay their debt to society. Rather they are forever stigmatized as "ex-cons" and, therefore, considered unreliable and dangerous by their neighbors, employers, fellow workers, and acquaintances. Also, they are harassed by the police as "likely suspects." The result is that they are often driven into a deviant subculture and eventually caught—about two-thirds are arrested within three years of leaving prison.

Progressives argue that conservative crime control measures are fundamentally flawed because they are "after the fact" solutions. Like a janitor mopping up the floor while the sink continues to overflow; he or she may even redouble the effort with some success but the source of the flooding has not been addressed. If I might mix metaphors here (although keeping with the aquatic theme), the obvious place to begin the attack on crime is *upstream*, before the criminal has been formed and the crimes have been committed.

We must concentrate our efforts on high-risk individuals before they become criminals (in particular, impoverished young inner city males). These prevention proposals take time, are very costly, and out-of-favor politically but they are the only realistic solutions to reduce violent street crime.

The problem with the conservative "after the fact" crime fighting proposals is that while promoting criminal justice, these programs dismantle social justice. Thus, they enhance a criminogenic climate. During the Reagan years, for example, $51 billion were removed from various poverty programs. Now, under the "Contract for America" the Republicans in Congress propose to reduce subsidized housing, to eliminate nutrition programs through WIC (Women, Infants, and Children), to let the states take care of subsidized school lunches, and to eliminate welfare for unmarried mothers under 18 who do not live with their parents or a responsible guardian.

Progressives argue that we abandon these children at our own peril. The current Republican proposals forsake the 26 percent of American children under six who live in poverty including 54 percent of all African American children and 44 percent of all Latino children under the age of six. Will we be safer as these millions of children in poverty grow to physical maturity?

Before I address specific solutions, I want to emphasize that sociologists examine the structural reasons for crime. This focus on factors outside the individual does not excuse criminal behavior, it tries to understand how certain structural factors *increase* the proportion of people who choose criminal options.

Knowing what we know about crime, the implications for policy are clear. These proposals, as you will note, are easy to suggest but they are very difficult to implement. I will divide my proposals into immediate actions to deal with crime now and long-term preventive measure:

1. The first step is to protect society from predatory sociopaths. This does not mean imprisoning more people. We should, rather, only imprison the truly dangerous. The criminal law should be redrawn so that the list of crimes reflects the real dangers that individuals pose to society. Since prison does more harm than good, we should provide reasonable alternatives such as house arrest, half-way houses, boot camps, electronic surveillance, job corps, and drug/alcohol treatment.

2. We must reduce the number of handguns and assault weapons by enacting and vigorously enforcing stringent gun controls at the federal level. The United States is an armed camp with 210 million guns in circulation. Jeffrey Reiman has put it this way:

"Trying to fight crime while allowing such easy access to guns is like trying to teach a child to walk and tripping him each time he stands up. In its most charitable light, it is hypocrisy. Less charitably, it is complicity in murder."

3. We must make a special effort to get guns out of the hands of juveniles. Research by James Wright and his colleagues at Tulane University found that juveniles are much more likely to have guns for protection than for status and power. They suggest that

we must restore order in the inner cities so that fewer young people do not feel the need to provide their own protection. They argue that a perceived sense of security by youth can be accomplished if there is a greater emphasis on community policing, more cooperation between police departments and inner city residents, and greater investment by businesses, banks, and cities in the inner city.

4. We must reinvent the criminal justice system so that it commands the respect of youth and adults. The obvious unfairness by race and social class must be addressed. Some laws are unfair. For example, the federal law requires a five-year, no-parole sentence for possession of five grams of crack cocaine, worth about $400. However, it takes 100 times as much powder cocaine—500 grams, worth $10,000—and a selling conviction to get the same sentence. Is this fair? Of course not. Is it racist? It is racist since crack is primarily used by African Americans while powder cocaine is more likely used by whites. There are also differences by race and social class in arrest patterns, plea bargain arrangements, sentencing, parole, and imposition of the death penalty. These differences provide convincing evidence that the poor and racial minorities are discriminated against in the criminal justice system. As long as the criminal justice system is perceived as unfair by the disadvantaged, that system will not exert any moral authority over them.

5. We must rehabilitate as many criminals as possible. Prisons should be more humane. Prisoners should leave prison with vocational skills useful in the real world. Prisoners should leave prison literate and with a high school degree. And, society should formally adopt the concept of "forgiveness" saying to ex-prisoners, in effect, you have been punished for your crime, we want you to begin a new life with a "clean" record.

6. We must legalize the production and sale of "illicit drugs" and treat addiction as a medical problem rather than a criminal problem. If drugs were legalized or decriminalized, crimes would be reduced in several ways: (a) By eliminating drug use as a criminal problem, we would have 1.12 million *fewer* arrests each year. (b) There would be many *fewer* prisoners (currently about 60 percent of all federal prisoners and 25 percent of all state prisoners are incarcerated for drug offenses). (c) Money now spent on the drug war ($31 billion annually, not counting prison construction) could be spent for other crime control programs such as police patrols, treatment of drug users, and jobs programs. (d) Drugs could be regulated and taxed, generating revenues of about $5

billion a year. (e) It would end the illicit drug trade that provides tremendous profits to organized crime, violent gangs, and other traffickers. (f) It would eliminate considerable corruption of the police and other authorities. (g) There would be many fewer homicides. Somewhere between one-fourth and one-half of the killings in the inner cities are drug-related. (h) The lower cost of purchasing drugs reduces the need to commit crimes to pay for drug habits.

*Long-term preventive measures to reduce violent crime:*

1. The link between poverty and street crime is indisputable. In the long run, reducing poverty will be the most effective crime fighting tool. Thus, as a society, we need to intensify our efforts to break the cycle of poverty. This means providing a universal and comprehensive health care system, low-cost housing, job training, and decent compensation for work. There must be pay equity for women. And, there must be an unwavering commitment to eradicate institutional sexism and racism. Among other benefits, such a strategy will strengthen families and give children resources, positive role models, and hope.

2. Families must be strengthened. Single-parent families and the working poor need subsidized child care, flexible work schedules, and leave for maternity and family emergencies at a reasonable proportion of their wages. Adolescent parents need the resources to stay in school. They need job training. We need to increase the commitment to family planning. This means providing contraceptives and birth control counseling to adolescents. This means using federal funds to pay for legal abortions when they are requested by poor women.

3. There must be a societal commitment to full and decent employment. Meaningful work at decent pay integrates individuals into society. It is a source of positive identity. Employed parents are respected by their children. Good paying jobs provide hope for the future. They also are essential to keep families together.

4. There must be a societal commitment to education. This requires two different programs. The first is to help at-risk children, beginning at an early age. As it is now, when poor children start school, they are already behind. As Sylvia Ann Hewlett has said:

"At age five, poor children are often less alert, less curious, and less effective at interacting with their peers than are more privileged youngsters."

This means that they are doomed to be underachievers. To overcome this we need intervention programs that prepare children for school. Research shows that Head Start and other programs can raise IQ scores significantly. There are two problems with Head Start, however. First, the current funding only covers 40 percent of eligible youngsters. And second, the positive effects from the Head Start program are sometimes short-lived because the children then attend schools that are poorly staffed, overcrowded, and ill-equipped.

This brings us to the second education program to help at-risk children. The government must equalize the resources of school districts, rather than the current situation where the wealth of school districts determines the amount spent per pupil. Actually, equalization is not the answer. I believe that there should be special commitment to invest *extra* resources in at-risk children. If we do, we will have a safer society in the long run.

These proposals seem laughable in the current political climate, where politicians—Republicans *and* Democrats—try to outdo each other in their toughness on crime and their disdain for preventive programs. They are wrong, however, and society is going to pay in higher crime rates in the future. I am convinced that the political agenda of the conservatives is absolutely heading us in the wrong direction—toward more violent crime rather than less.

The proposals that I have suggested are based on what we sociologists know about crime. They should be taken seriously, but they are not. The proposals are also based on the assumption that if we can give at-risk young people hope, they will become a part of the community rather than alienated from it. My premise is this: Everyone needs a dream. Without a dream, we become apathetic. Without a dream, we become fatalistic. Without a dream, and the hope of attaining it, society becomes our enemy. Many young people act in antisocial ways because they have lost their dream. These troubled and troublesome people are society's creations because we have not given them the opportunity to achieve their dreams—instead society has structured the situation so that they will fail. Until they feel that they have a stake in society, they will fail, and so will we.

# IMPACT OF THE MASS MEDIA

## TELEVISION NEWS REPORTING[1]
### ANDREW A. ROONEY[2]

Andy Rooney is well known for his humorous and often acerbic comments delivered at the end of the popular weekly television program "60 Minutes" and also in his syndicated newspaper column. Both on television and in his column, Rooney often uses humor to call attention to serious concerns of viewers and readers.

In October 1994, Rooney was invited to address the annual meeting of the Radio and Television News Directors Association. The Association is a professional society of news department executives in broadcast, cable, and network organizations. In his speech, Rooney chose to discuss the decline in standards of both network and local television news, although he acknowledged that the members of his audience had probably heard more on this topic then they wished. "Unfortunately," he said, "even if you don't want to hear it, it's a subject that's impossible to avoid so that's what I'm going to talk about."

Early in the address, Rooney referred to CBS news anchorman Dan Rather's speech given to the same organization at its meeting a year earlier. (For Rather's speech and reports of reactions to it, see *Representative American Speeches 1993–1994*.)

Rooney gave his speech before about 350 RTNDA members at the Los Angeles Convention Center. He was introduced by his daughter, Emily, an Association director, and his son Brian, an ABC news correspondent.

*Mr. Rooney's speech:* Thank you. At the outset I want to say that I don't think you want to hear one more person talk about the decline in standards of both network and local television news.

Unfortunately, even if you don't want to hear it, it's a subject that's impossible to avoid so that's what I'm going to talk about.

[1]Delivered to the Radio and Television News Directors Association at their annual convention at the Los Angeles Convention Center in Los Angeles on October 12, 1994.

[2]For biographical note see Appendix.

I mean, that's the tradition here, isn't it? We talk about how bad we're doing? We don't do anything about it. Did Ed Murrow's speech solve all our problems? Are things better since Dan Rather laid it all out last year in his good speech?

I don't want to be too broad in my criticism of television news. I want to talk specifically about anchormen and the decline and fall of reporting. I thought that would be fun.

Most of us assume we're all operating with the same set of standards for news but that may not be true. If it is true, it's hard to account for the decline.

Ancient Greece and Rome didn't go into a decline because there was anything wrong with the principles on which their civilizations were based. They went into a decline because the people who believed in those principles became a minority and they were overrun by people who didn't understand those principles at all. To some extent that has happened in the news business.

I speak mostly about network news. When I travel, I always watch, no matter what city I'm in and I've seen some good local news broadcasts and I've seen some bad ones.

It seems the bigger the city, the worse the local news. Local news in New York tends to be poor because it has such a huge constituency, it doesn't know which element of the constituency to appeal to.

Maybe the decline in television reporting started when we began using the term "investigative reporting." Up until that time, all reporting had been "investigative." "Investigative reporting" is redundant.

I concede there's a semantic problem here.

The word reporter, in its literal sense, suggests someone who only passes on news but, in the newspaper business, a reporter has always been someone who first sought out the information.

We may need a word we don't have, a word for the person in television who seeks out information and then writes it and presents it in an interesting and informative way.

In television now, anchormen are reporters only to the extent that they report news that other people have collected. They announce what the news is without ever having independently found out any of it themselves. They are news announcers and it's ridiculous that they're paid what they are for that kind of work.

They ought to be ashamed of themselves but they aren't. They're proud of themselves.

It's wrong to use a good reporter as an announcer. The best example I know of that is Dan Rather. He proved recently in

Haiti, as he's proven so often before, that he's one of the best reporters in the business. It seems to me the job of reading the news could be done by someone with less talent.

This is true of Brokaw and Jennings. They're both first rate reporters. They ought to be out there, away from a desk and the teleprompter, gathering information and telling us what they've found. Anytime a good reporter is made an anchorman, it's a step in the wrong direction.

Anchormen have become too important to television news. You look at a news broadcast and who and what the anchorman or anchorwoman is, their personal idiosyncracies, often dominate the information they pass on.

We know how our anchorman cocks his head; we recognize where he came from because of his accent. We judge the anchorwoman has on too much or not enough makeup tonight. We comment that he looks a little flaky tonight or that his hair is not as grey as it was last night. We note she's as good looking as Diane Sawyer or, more probably, nowhere near as good-looking as Diane.

Too often anchormen are playing the part of actors and good actors are a dime a dozen. There are a thousand actors within five miles of where we sit, waiting for one writer to put something down on paper so they can get the job of saying it on camera. There isn't a good Hollywood actor alive who couldn't sit in the anchormen's chair tomorrow and do a good job reading the news without knowing Somalia from Haiti.

It's very difficult for any of us in the business of appearing on camera to keep from becoming actors. Years ago I did a one hour documentary on the bureaucracy in Washington. It was one of the first long pieces I did on camera myself. I sat at my desk doing a long description of how a bureaucrat rewrites the specifications for a job in order to give an old friend a job.

"Say you want to hire your old college roommate," I said, and at that point I leaned way back in my chair. I hadn't intended to, I just did.

I finished what I was saying, in about a minute. The cameraman said "Andy, that was just great. It looked so natural when you leaned back. I didn't know you were going to do it and I lost a little of the top of your head. Do that once more for me just the way you did it, you know, real natural." I knew at that moment how hard it was going to be to keep from becoming an actor.

What we need from our anchormen is a little anonymity. It should not make a damn bit of difference who's reading the news to us. It does make a difference who the reporter is because, if he did the story we have to know what his slant is apt to be and how reliable he is.

I don't think the anchormen would disagree with me about this, either. They're pretty good guys, at least two of them are. I have some reservations about the third.

Each one of them would be happy to do honest work again as a reporter if it could be done in a way that didn't make it look as though he or she got fired.

I was trying to figure the other day—I think there are now nine people in television news who make more than $3 million. Most are anchormen or women for one show or another.

Please don't try to make your own list on your napkin while I'm talking.

To tell you the truth, I'm surprised that the owners or CEO's of the television networks haven't taken their cue from pro football and put in a salary cap for correspondents. The owners of professional football teams did it a couple of years ago and it's been wonderful for them. Each team can spend only $35 million on players' salaries.

There are roughly as many correspondents at a network as there are football players on a team.

I can imagine network executives saying "My gosh. Why didn't WE think of a salary cap for network news, for the correspondents own good, of course.

Each news division would be allowed to spend only a limited amount on correspondents. It could be dangerous for high paid anchormen I suppose. I mean, to make room for new talent, Peter Jennings might end up just another Phil Simms.

Of course, I know how a salary cap would work in real life in the television news business. If there were 60 correspondents, the anchorman would get $34 million and the remaining million would be divided among the other 59 correspondents.

Something happens to anchormen after they've had the job for about five years. It isn't their fault but it ultimately affects their news judgment, their judgment of the world around them, and their judgment of themselves. I have an idea that would change all that.

We've all heard the debate over term limitations for Congressmen. A lot of people think they should serve just one term and then go home. I don't know about politicians but here and now I propose a six-year term limitation on anchormen.

This would be for local as well as network anchormen and women. Six years and out.

Retroactive!

I don't want to lay all of this on anchormen. I'm not satisfied with the job the correspondents are doing, either. A long while ago, television started calling its reporters "correspondents."

Most of what they report is not reporting at all but what would be called rewrite on a newspaper. There are damn few stories on the evening news on the average night that involve any original reporting.

A lot of network correspondents suffer from the anchorman syndrome. They are no longer reporters, that is, they don't go out looking for stories, and it isn't their fault. The producers in New York meet in the morning, decide what the stories are and tell the correspondents. The correspondents then go out and look for something to stand in front of while they tell the story. They often get their information from the same place everyone does, the newspaper. The desk doesn't want to be confused with a lot of facts that don't concur with their opinion of what the story is. They have a show to get on the air.

More and more correspondents are hanging around the office until someone on the desk asks them to go to a trial, a fire, an earthquake, or a war and stand in front of that. If the fire gets real big, the correspondents in the field don't get to cover it. The anchorman himself shows up—presumably because the trial, or the fire, or the earthquake, or the war, is too big for the correspondent on the scene to handle.

The anchorman elbows the correspondent out of the way and says "Here, I'll do that."

In the correspondents' defense, I'd have to say that the reason they aren't out digging up their own stories is, the network finds it too expensive to pay them while they look, especially if it involves a camera crew. Getting a story can take time and even after spending time, a good reporter won't always come back with something. It's cheaper to wait until something comes in on the wire or appears in the newspaper and take it from there.

There are a small handful of people at each network who *are* allowed to do some of their own reporting and their's is the best stuff we see. Some of them are beat reporters. I could name ten people who do very good, original reports but there are probably fifteen so I'm not going to. Bob Simon and Jim Wooten are favorites of mine.

When I first looked for work at CBS News in 1949, I came to the news director, a man named Ted Church with a simple idea. I wanted to work in his news room on the telephone gathering bits and pieces of information over the phone that would flesh out the stories that had arrived there from other sources.

There was a great city editor of the *New York Herald Tribune,* Joe Hertzberg. Joe knew New York so well that when a flash came in about some incident, he could tell from the address what block it was in anywhere in New York. He'd go to the phone book, find someone who lived in that block, and call to try to get a first hand report.

That's a job that, as far as I know, still doesn't exist.

I wish the writing was better on television news but you can't have good writing in seven seconds or even nine.

Writing for television is different than writing for print and there's no way they'll ever come together. I started my career writing for other people and you quickly learn what the problem is. No one speaks as he writes and no one writes as he speaks. What you have to do is find some middle-ground. You use the language in a way that isn't as stiff as formal writing and isn't as loose as conversation. There's no time for good writing.

All three networks have especially able business correspondents but I don't think television news, local or network, but especially local, has done a good job reporting on business. I guess that's often because the station owner is a local businessman.

If he isn't, he's a close friend of most of the business people in town and investigative work by his reporters doesn't make him popular over at the club.

There are a great many stories about business and businesses that are going uncovered. Business is difficult, I know that. It's difficult because business is more secretive than the CIA. Television news has always done a better job as a watchdog of government than of business.

I think it's easier to report the evils of government than the evils of business. There aren't any more bad guys in government, they're just easier to find. There are laws like the Freedom of Information Act that work in a reporter's favor reporting on government. There's no Freedom of Information Act for business.

Larry Tisch has never called me to ask for my business advice. I guess he knows I'm busy. He doesn't want to bother me but I do have an idea for Larry, Howard Stringer, and Eric Ober, my bosses.

Here's my suggestion. Now, I'm fitting this idea to CBS because I know CBS best but it could be at any of the other networks. It might appeal to Rupert Murdoch.

The reason it would be best at CBS or Fox is, they're not so much run by a corporation and a board of trustees as they are run by one man. Murdoch or Tisch don't have to raise their hands if they want to leave the room.

Larry is a very wealthy man with good instincts. He's given a great deal of money to good causes. Why wouldn't it appeal to him to set out to build the greatest news organization there has ever been—dwarf in size and quality the *Associated Press*, the *New York Times*, the *Washington Post*, the *Los Angeles Times*, *The Wall Street Journal*, *Time*, *Life*, *Newsweek*, and all the networks. Ignore the money and set out to make a name for himself as the greatest benefactor of public information there has ever been.

It's my feeling that he'd get richer than ever if he did this but say he didn't. Why wouldn't he spend the money just for the fun of it. The thrill of knowing you were doing something great. If he liked, he could call it the Tisch News Network, TNN. Sort of catchy.

If I were Larry, I'd start with a very dramatic move. Take "60 Minutes" off the air Sunday nights. Announce to his affiliates that, whether they liked it or not, CBS would present a one-hour news broadcast every night of the week from nine pm until ten pm.

It wouldn't be taken out of the local stations' news time. It would be taken out of entertainment programming time. He'd guarantee local stations the same money they're getting now for situation comedies.

He would take all twenty-one "60 Minutes" producers and assign them to the show. Each of the five "60 Minutes" correspondents who do the reports would do one fifteen minutes piece a week, one correspondent each night.

He'd hire the best reporters, the best producers, the best camera crews. Forget the bottom line. What possible use could he put a few billion dollars to than one great hour of news every night.

He'd shut down all the spinoff magazine shows like "48 Hours" and "Nose To Nose With Connie Chung" and put all those good people to work on the one hour evening news. The way it is now at the networks, every time a correspondent does a good job on their regular half hour news broadcast, they take the person off it and put him or her on a magazine show. Maybe Larry would like to hire back all the good people CBS has lost to ABC.

Reopen the bureaus that have been shut down in the United States and abroad. Do everything right to make it a great news organization. Hewitt's getting bored with the success of "60 Minutes." Make him the overall producer.

I fail to understand why one of the networks hasn't found it possible and profitable to go to an hour of news each night.

One of the most disappointing things about free enterprise and our capitalist system is that it seems to discourage quality in the production of anything. Has any product *ever* been improved when a big company took over a small one? Is NBC news better since GE took over NBC? There's no question that the trend in almost every business enterprise for as long as any of us can remember, has been away from quality.

This has been unfortunately true with television news. There's simply no question about it.

News is important. You people in the news business are important. News is the way most people arrive at the truth about things. The biggest trouble the world has is lack of information and misinformation. Informed intelligence is the only hope we have for solving the world's problems. Ultimately we in the news business have to hope and believe we have more to do with who people vote for than the candidates' political speeches have.

We have to believe that if all the truth were known about everything by everyone, it would be a better world. That's why news is important and the digging out of facts is what makes reporting important.

Dick Salant said that journalism is a business enterprise but it is a moral enterprise, too. I liked that a lot and I'd like to see everyone who doesn't think so get out.

And one last thing, on that nightly one hour news broadcast, I'd have a desk in the studio and I'd be free to break into the show anytime I felt like it. My spot would be called "Wait a Damn Minute with Andy Rooney."

---

ELECTRIC RHETORIC:
THE TRANSFORMATION
OF AMERICAN POLITICAL TALK[1]
Bruce E. Gronbeck[2]

---

Many colleges and universities in the United States have endowed lectureships that enable them to bring distinguished schol-

[1]Delivered at the Salter Concert Hall, Wabash College in Crawfordsville, Indiana on March 24, 1994 at 8:00 p.m.
[2]For biographical note see Appendix.

ars and leaders to the campus to deliver public addresses. The lectures often are reprinted and distributed to former colleagues, students, and alumni.

One such series is the Brigance Forum at Wabash College in Crawfordsville, Indiana. The Forum is an annual public lecture or debate in memory of William Norwood Brigance, teacher, scholar, and leader in the Speech Association of America. In his thirty-eight years at Wabash, and through his textbooks, he taught thousands of college and high school students to be more effective when they spoke. Professionally, he was well known as the editor of the first two volumes of the pioneer *History and Criticism of American Public Address* and as editor of the *Quarterly Journal of Speech*. He also served as president of the Speech Association of America.

The lecturer for the 1994 Brigance Forum was Bruce E. Gronbeck, chairman of the Communications Department at the University of Iowa and, at the time, president of the Speech Communication Association, a sixty-three hundred member professional association for members and practitioners of the various communication arts and sciences.

In his lecture, Professor Gronbeck chose to address the subject of how electronic discoveries and developments had affected public discourse.

Gronbeck presented the lecture to an audience of approximately two hundred students, faculty, and townspeople on March 24, 1995, at 8:00 p.m. in the Salter Concert Hall on campus. A dinner to honor senior speech majors and debaters preceded his remarks. Wabash faculty member Joe O'Rourke noted, "The annual lecture has become a significant event not only on campus, but to our alumni and colleagues who receive the printed version each year."

*Mr. Gronbeck's speech:* It is an honor for me to have been asked to address this forum. William Norwood Brigance, like so many others, came out of South Dakota to the University of Iowa because of its Ph.D. program in rhetoric and public address. Thanks to the accident of alphabetization—B came before the L in Floyd Wesley Lambertson's last name—Brigance is memorialized as Iowa's first Ph.D. in rhetorical studies, class of 1930. He had the honor as well of being A. Craig Baird's first successful doctoral advisee. My personal connection with him goes back to 1959. That's when I took my first college course in public speaking; the textbook we used was his *Speech: Its Techniques and Disciplines in a*

*Free Society.* It was a wonderful book because it grounded speech skills in a broadly liberal arts orientation; it had chapters on public opinion and its scientific as well as rhetorical management, the rights of listeners in a democratic society, ethics, the history of rhetoric, and "dynamic persuasion in an industrial democracy." Even now, when I have taken over the writing of a textbook done by one of Brigance's rivals—Alan Monroe from just up the road in West Lafayette—I still think of the liberal arts emphasis that Brigance built into his pedagogy, the passion with which he debated over the democratizing power of unions, and his commitment to the search for truth in public life. He guides my work even today and I'm honored to be lecturing in his name.

Indeed, this evening I take my text from the foreword to his 1952 book on public speaking. In that foreword, he is concerned about what we now call the mass culture theses: the propositions that grew out of the post-World War II explosion of the United States economy, population, and consumption of radio, television, and film. In wishing to counter intellectual attacks on anything or anyone who was "popular," Brigance wrote:

In a free society the speaker's compulsion is to be "popular," if by that derogatory term it is meant to be understood by the masses. But to be "popular" does not mean to be careless in reasoning, weak in judgment, or irresponsible in talk. It means to be understood by the people. This is a distinction that students must be taught to recognize, and to which they should be held accountable from the beginning.

In associating that which is popular, especially in politics, with that which flows to and from the public, the populace, Brigance was implicitly doing battle with such social critics as Ernest van den Haag and Dwight MacDonald, who foresaw the destruction of civilization in the wake of television. Not so Brigance. He had a clear vision even as television antennas were beginning their spread across the face of this country. Let me quote from Chapter 21 of that 1952 textbook:

Radio and television are not mere scientific inventions. They are agents of revolution that are profoundly influencing the operating nature of democracy. . . . They eliminated at last the barriers of both time and space. . . . They have made possible an alert and informed citizenry regardless of the size of a nation, even in an area as vast as the United States. . . . [R]adio and television have increased the power of the mass of people.

Now, it must be admitted that, just perhaps, Brigance's vision was a bit overblown. From 1960 to 1988, this country saw an erosion in the percentage of its eligible voters casting ballots in the presidential election, reaching a 64-year low of 50.1 percent in the Bush-Dukakis confrontation. As well, media critics of the likes of Neil Postman talk about American politics as "peekaboo" politics: a series of short, hit-and-run stories that emphasize the visual more than the substantive aspects of social issues and public policy. Communications scholar Robert Denton has argued that American "teledemocracy" is in serious trouble because of the stranglehold television has on political process and decision making.

Having said that, however, in no way disturbs Brigance's points: that for better or worse political operations in a democracy come down to decisions the people make, and that the electronic media have served more to empower than to disenfranchise the people. Tonight I want to agree with Iowa's first Ph.D. in rhetoric, as I extend his analysis. After forty-two more years of experience with mass media and politics, I think we're in a position to carry the Wabash professor's arguments forward. While Brigance may have been overly optimistic, he had the description of American politics in the era of mass media essentially correct. More specifically, I want to do four things tonight: (1) Talk briefly about the assumptions of American politics before the coming of electronic media, (2) mention the forces of change that beset and, as Brigance argued, revolutionized American politics, (3) try to describe concisely the characteristics of political communication in our time, and finally (4) conclude with both praise for and warning about what we face as a political culture in the electronic age.

In my short time tonight, I will discuss only three of the significant features of the classic American democratic system of government—features we've been accused of destroying in the electronic age. Those features are *rhetorical rationality, political disinterestedness,* and *social melting-pottism.*

The greatest teacher I ever took a course from, A. Craig Baird, wrote much about the power and rationality of good political rhetoric. He wrote about it from an inherited political ideology, the 19th-century liberal-pluralist conception of democracy. Of political speechmaking, Baird wrote that it "is a natural and wholesome consequent of the form of polity under which we live. In deliberation and decision, the democratic way provides for the exchange of views; the oral transmission of ideas is a rightful prerogative of the man who enjoys the estate of free discussion." Baird taught at least three generations of American political-rhetorical analysts that well-reasoned speeches were the primary tools of democratic process. He taught us that the words of great men—assuredly men—were the tools of gentry oligarchies, that sustained pieces of political reasoning ought to satisfy not only the needs of the moment but the political demands of all time— which is to say, to be both timely and timeless.

As Neil Postman has noted, the great political discourse of the 18th and parts of the 19th centuries that Baird so loved was highly literate, crafted for eras that prized *eloquentia* and long, sustained arguments. William Pitt and Charles James Fox in St. Stephen's Chapel, John J. Calhoun and Daniel Webster in the Senate chamber—these great British and American political orators assumed the broad view even while constructing syllogistic arguments with validity and point. Their speeches were full of classical allusion and poetry. Their words were meant to be read as well as heard. They were the products of men whose consciousness was dominated by print.

As well, a kind of disinterestedness was assumed to characterize the politician in both 18th-century England and 19th-century America. To be sure, politicians wished to advance within the ranks of government, but anyone found to be making personal gain from public employment could be and occasionally actually was censured. One of the arguments, of course, for drawing politicians from the propertied and monied classes was that they would not be tempted to pursue politics for personal betterment. They often thought of themselves as even independent from their constituents. Thus, in 1774 oratorical giant Edmund Burke characterized the role of a member of parliament in this manner:

[H]is unbiased opinion, his mature judgment, his enlightened conscience, he ought not to sacrifice to you, to any man, or to any set of men living. These he does not derive from your pleasure; no, nor from the law and the constitution. They are a trust from Providence, for the abuse of which he is deeply answerable. Your representative owes you, not his industry only, but his judgment; and he betrays, instead of serving you, if he sacrifices it to your opinion.

Here, the view of disinterestedness is transcendent: Burke owes no allegiance to special interests or even to his electors, but only to God and Parliament itself.

A third important characteristic of traditional American political understanding is its commitment to what I call melting-pottism. Nowhere is it better illustrated than on the Statue of Liberty. The statue was immortalized two years before its arrival from France in Emma Lazarus's poem, "The New Colossus." Inscribed on the pedestal of the statue were these words:

> Give me your tired, your poor,
> Your huddled masses yearning to breathe free,
> The wretched refuse of your teeming shore,
> Send these, the homeless, tempest-tost to me,
> I lift my lamp beside the golden door!

Together with Israel Zanwill's 1908 play, "The Melting Pot," and the construction of American identity on its coins in the phrase *epluribus unam,* "out of many, one," our classic political ideology assumed we always could homogenize immigrants into a dominant set of values that, in turn, could serve as uncontested terms in political argument. Daniel Webster could appeal to "Union and Liberty" in 1850, U.S. Immigration could term potential citizens "huddled masses yearning to breathe free" even while stripping them of their own history and building their future political orientations for them, and Albert Beveridge could end the 19th century reciting America's shared political virtues in his imperialistic "March of the Flag" speech because of powerful, shared values. Melting-pottism, at bottom, meant that political dialogue was consensus-building, with consensus possible because of a fund of political and social capital we all presumably held in common.

Traditional American democratic thought thus assumed we could engineer binding agreements through group representatives who, because of their wealth and position, would speak for—even instead of—their constituents with disinterestedness yet vision, and, together with other aristocratic politicians, would come after a literate debate to proper political decisions organized around generally agreed upon beliefs, attitudes, and values. While this vision was under sometimes weak, sometimes strong, attack for most of this century, it became irreversibly defocused in 1952.

Technically, if you want to do a full history of electronic mass media and their role in politics, you have to start in 1924, when Calvin Coolidge's folks made the first campaign film and when radio broadcast the first political conventions. But, I think 1952 was the truly definitive year, for that's when a television network reporter, Walter Cronkite, became a familiar fixture in American living rooms. CBS led the way in showing the other networks how to cover the drama of American political conventions. That same year, the first television ads for presidential candidates appeared.

Dwight Eisenhower showed us how to advertise, spending between $800,000 and $1.5 million on television spots—about ten to twenty times the $77,000 spent by his opponent, Adlai Stevenson.

The year 1960 was equally important. The Kennedy-Nixon campaign was saturated by television: the Kennedy interviews in West Virginia, which neutralized his religion in a staunchly Protestant state; the Democratic convention, which brother Bobby turned into a media show place; the Kennedy-Nixon debates, where Kennedy's short, crisp, self-assured answers were in marked contrast to the labored, overly reasoned remarks of Nixon. Another technique the Kennedys perfected was the staged media event. To get good news shots, two accomplices would hold an airport crowd back with a rope. Then, when Kennedy started down the stairs of the plane, they would drop the rope, letting the crowd surge to and around the candidate, all recorded by TV cameras for that evening's news.

The 1960 election was important for another technological reason: the computer entered politics decisively. The computerized census data of 1960 were used by the Kennedys to trace public attitudes and the movements of peoples around from the country—the shrinking rural vote, the growth of suburbs, the abandonment of city centers. They used computerized data to help them select issues. As well, Bobby Kennedy hired on Joe Napolitan, a pollster, and Larry O'Brien, a political manager with a sense for the press. Together, they showed the world of presidential politics how to work a three-step formula to success: "1. Decide how you want the voter to feel or react. 2. Decide what to do to make him react that way. 3. Do it." It was Napolitan who argued early on that in a day of electronic media, it is a candidate's personal qualities more than his stands on issues that usually win the day.

Television and the computer, therefore, certainly became the two primary forces behind the development of electrified political discourse. Over the last quarter century, thanks to the advent of electronic media as well as some financial reforms and party restructuring, Americans have lived through absolutely fundamental changes in presidential politics. Television has given us whole new kinds of political messages and whole new perspectives on the electoral process. Computerization has speeded up campaigning even while helping to extend that campaign to ridiculous lengths. Overall, the Neoclassical vision of gentrified politicians calmly deliberating important issues long enough to solve problems has been replaced by electric bursts of hot-pink rhetoric pulsating through audiences outlined by computer inkjets.

Now then, before we can understand and evaluate contemporary, electronically powered political talk, we must examine at least briefly some of its most important features. I have time to deal with three concepts:

*1. Rhetorical condensation.* Paradoxically, even as the sheer amount of political information available publicly increases—thanks to computers, satellites, and the decreased costs of distribution—citizens sense that they lack the requisite political knowledge to understand the issues and to make good electoral decisions. In campaigns, we are awash in 10-, 30-, and 60-second political ads and five-to-ten second sound bites on the news, but to little avail. The politicians are everywhere, the news, talk shows, CNN interviews, and C-SPAN broadcasts, and yet citizens complain that politicians talk about the wrong issues or about the right issues in a language that is not comprehensible. Citizens find themselves confronted with what is sometimes called "professional speak"—a special, inside-the-Capitol-Hill-beltway argot that makes no sense in Dubuque, Iowa, or Crawfordsville, Indiana.

Now let me be clear here: the shortened message, what I call rhetorical condensation, is not new. Aristotle discussed the maxim in Book II of the *Rhetoric*. He suggested the maxim was a guide to prudential conduct, the conclusion of a kind of audience-centered reasoning pattern he called the enthymeme. The maxim to Aristotle had two rhetorical advantages to recommend it: it could compel assent from audiences because it was built on views they already held, and it could invest discourse with moral character. So, for example, when I talk of "government of the people, by the people, and for the people," I call up or evoke a view of democracy you're familiar with and I let you know I stand with Abraham Lincoln, the most moral president Americans can think of. That's why maxims are effective. Maxims have been a part of western politics since ancient Greece and Rome.

There's a difference in the sound bite or the video clip of today, however. Not only does it reach beyond the verbal in its use of sound and picture, but it is often all we are given as bases for political decisions. Aristotle saw the maxim as but one part of the communication process, but today it is often the whole message: abstracted for the six o'clock news, flashed in a short ad, or mounted in huge type on a billboard. Furthermore, thanks to the

American public's education into the ways of film and television, we've gotten used to fast-paced editing, power-packed soundtracks, and fleeting pictures. New York Governor Mario Cuomo has put it as well as anyone:

Sticking by your principles requires that you explain your principles, and in this age of electronic advocacy this process can often be tedious and frustrating. This is especially so when you must get your message across in twenty-eight-second celluloid morsels, when images prove often more convincing than ideas. Labels are no longer a tendency in our politics. In this electronic age, they are our politics.

So today, effective political communication between leaders and the led depends upon the memorable phrase, set in a visual swirl of icons and a soundtrack straight off MTV. That's rhetorical condensation.

*2. Narrative logic.* While you can find some fully blown arguments on "Meet the Press" or C-SPAN interviews, much of the political talk you hear today is narrativized—given to you in story form. Somehow, in a scientized, complicated, distant, enormous society of over 260 million people with a four-trillion dollar debt to their names, an anecdote about an African American in Tupelo or a little old lady in Peoria is reassuring. Through such stories in our political discourses we learn that individuals count, that the abstract can be concretized in the lives of particular people, and that complicated political situations can be reduced to simple morality plays.

Indeed, we've turned much of our politics into not only stories but sociodramas—plays that are acted out for us on the evening news. Again, Aristotle long ago recognized that speakers must make their "own character look right" and put their "hearers, who are to decide, into the right frame of mind." He told us specifically that speakers must demonstrate their good sense, their good will, and their good moral character if they're to be effective political advocates. We've now, however, taken such advice to an extreme. We expect our politicians to be good actors, good performers, if they're to be thought competent, probably because we now can actually see them acting out their political performances right in our own living rooms.

Just look at the political news stories that fill our television screens this spring. We're watching the story of Whitewater, which is presented to us as the story of greed and ambition that may well bring the great down, a pure, unadulterated Greek tragedy. We have good seats at the battle over health care in America, where little people without insurance are doing battle with the Goliaths of the insurance and medical establishments, a great melodrama where we can cheer for the little St. Georges who are trying to slay the dragons of our time. The stories of Bill Clinton's eating, Iowa Congressman Jim Nussle's paper bag over his head, Senator Bob Packwood's sex-filled diaries, and Attorney General Janet Reno's padded shoulders and polyester wardrobe are all comedies in a classical sense, plays with characters whose personal foibles critique some of the sociopolitical rules of today. These comedies are not always funny, just ask Packwood, but they always are an important kind of social commentary.

As Wisconsin political scientist Murray Edelman has argued, "The construction of a spectacle and everyday political action are the same thing, though the pretence that they are separate helps legitimize official actions." By that he means that citizens have come to expect politicians cast as characters, usually, of course, heroic or villainous characters, in political morality plays, probably so that we can think of politicians as moral people rather than as, well, politicians. I suspect also that Americans have come to rely on such stories or plays in their politics because narrative forms have dominated their lives for much of this century. The film, radio drama, and television storytelling of the twentieth century has immersed each of us in a narrative social universe. Your consumption of mass media has made storytelling and playacting integral to the way you live your lives. And so it is little wonder that political decision making is governed by what I'm calling narrative logic, a reasoning pattern, not based on syllogisms and scientific inductions, but on characters acting morally for the benefit of the community.

3. *Evoked meaning.* The third characteristic of electrified political talk that I think is terribly important is what I'll call evoked meaning tonight. As words have been devalued politically, as pictures and sound have taken on more importance in electronic media, and as Americans have come to spend more and more of their time in front of the television set: it's on seven hours a day in the average household—we have come to rely on a new method of meaning-making in our political system. We've learned how to interpret meanings that have not actually been articulated. Instead, they are *evoked,* that is, called up out of us, out of our shared experiences.

To show you what I'm talking about, let me play two ads from the presidential campaign of 1988: the so-called "revolving door"

ad built by Republicans and the so-called "empty chair" ad built
by Democrats. Now, notice something odd but important: the
messages of these ads—"Mike Dukakis is soft on crime and would
be a dangerous president" and "George Bush does not take his
political responsibilities to the people seriously"—are not actually
said or even shown in the ads themselves. What do we get in the
revolving door? We get six factual statements about Dukakis's
actions as governor and his desire to do for America what he did
for Massachusetts and one ambiguous value judgment: "America
can't afford that risk." The pictures show us a darkening sky,
prison guards, a revolving door, and a little photo of Bush. The
soundtrack has the narrator's voice and music produced by a
synthesizer: a kind of drum beat, a sort of music, and an electronic tone that flattens out to a hum by the end. Nowhere does the ad
say or show us that Dukakis's mistakes brought kidnapping and
rape into others' lives or that he'd probably do so again as president. You, the viewer, supply those ideas; the ad draws them out
of you.

That's what I mean by evoked meaning. The revolving door
ad plays off your association of criminality with darkness and
prisons, your fear of criminal recidivism from having seen too
many movies and TV programs about escaped felons, your association of the commercial's soundtrack with a kind of music used
to depict criminal activity on cop shows, and your experience with
failed state and federal programs. The pictures are given power
by the words and the sounds; the sounds have their meanings
directed by your experience; and the words become emotionally
charged by pictures and sounds. In other words, in electric political rhetoric, meanings are not contained "in" the communication
channels of words, sounds, and pictures; meanings are constructed by viewers who have learned to blend the messages from
those channels.

The children raised on *Sesame Street* now watch MTV. Their
parents were generally raised with television as part of their lives.
The last two generations have been taught by their television
experiences to "read" television codes, visual codes, as easily, as
normally, as the generation before that was taught to read literate
codes. As a result of such life experiences, meaning-making is as
much an evocative process as it was an assertive process decades
ago. We have learned to understand not only what has been said,
but what has been called up in the process of that saying. And
that's why all of us knew the revolving door ad was an attack on

Dukakis and the empty chair was an attack on Bush and Quayle. The Democrats didn't have to say that vice presidential selections are vitally important and that Dan Quayle is unqualified to be president. You *knew* that's what those ads were saying because you're a sophisticated decoder of television messages.

Now then, if we take the three characteristics of electric political rhetoric together, we get the following view of contemporary politics. American politics in the late twentieth century is an exercise in storytelling or dramatic enactment, where the leading characters, the politicians and those they speak about, are cast in roles of heroes and villains, as they act out morality plays the citizens can understand because of their experience with electronic mass media. Political messages themselves are short and emotion-laden; that's all they need be because the citizens of an electronic age know how to decode the fragments of political talk they're presented with. Electronic political talk, in all of its visual and phonic complexity, evokes meanings from citizens trained to assemble those meanings out of their shared knowledges, their shared past.

As I get ready to close this all-too-short peek at electric rhetoric, I would like to suggest what I see as both the strengths and the sociomoral weaknesses of the communication practices of our own time.

First, I would emphasize that we simply cannot turn the clock back. There are those, such as Neil Postman, who make a good living telling us that we ought to return to the 18th century, when great politicians talked beautifully. Well folks, we can't. You can talk back to your television set, but few of you would actually throw it out. You can moan about your inability to use a computer to its fullest, but it's impossible to make it through this life armed only with a No. 2 pencil and a yellow legal pad. Technologies per se are neither good nor bad; it's the way they get used, the way a society trains us to employ them, that needs critique.

Second, however, we must recognize that new communication technologies alter both the way societies are put together and the way we think about our selves. So, ancient oral cultures were tribal; ideas could be shared only face-to-face in oral cultures, and individuals really had identities only as parts of those groups. The coming of writing, however, changed all that. It became possible to transport messages over great distances, so that empires could replace tribes as the major mechanisms for social organization. As well, you could write yourself on a piece of paper, separating your voice from your body with a quill pen; writing allowed senses of self to be recorded and inspected. Writing, in other words, changed both social organization and one's sense of self-identity.

Just as literate cultures replaced oral cultures, so is an electronic culture replacing the older literate cultures. Replacement is too strong a word, of course, because both oral exchange and literate communication coexist with the telephone and television in our time. Yet, it cannot be denied that the electronic media are the dominant media—and hence are, heaven help us, affecting our sense of social structure and self-image. President Bush's articulation of a New World Order depended upon a web of electronic media to hold the nations of the world together. Or, as another example, those of you who spend your time surfing on computer bulletin boards, where you can talk about almost anything you want with people from around the world, with each of you assuming whatever kind of self-identity you want, know that the electronic age is changing our social structures and even individual psyches.

It should come as no surprise, then, that this era also has revolutionized our politics. I currently know a young man in Iowa City running for the county board of supervisors principally through a computer network. I can log on to the university computer everyday to find news items and campaign issues flowing from his keyboard to my screen; if I'm willing to serve as an electronic campaigner, he'll log me onto a second service that allows him to communicate with his workers on a daily basis. The only face-to-face work he suggests this team do is drink beer at a local watering hole every couple of weeks to make sure everyone's happy. You still can't pour beer through a fiber optic cable. The point is, politics at all levels is now steeped in electric circuitry and it has changed fundamentally because of that fact.

Third, this is not all bad. Thanks to television and computers, you as a voter have much, much more information available from many more sources than your grandparents had. You know more than they did. You are a more sophisticated processor of political information than they were. You are much more likely to hold politicians accountable for their actions than even your parents; having the Watergate scandal piped into our living rooms every night for almost two years is one of the reasons that the Whitewater scandal is playing so well right now. Television has destroyed the distance between Washington, DC, and Washington, Iowa.

Television, as Josh Meyrowitz reminds us, lets us sit at *sidestage* to political dramas, being neither frontstage as audience nor backstage as workers, but sidestage—able to view the event and yet interpret it in a detached kind of way. And that makes you a better citizen in a democracy. Remember what Brigance said.

Yet, fourth, while I think we have much to celebrate in electric political rhetoric and its liberating effects, I know we have plenty to worry about as well. The French social critic Jean Baudrillard calls contemporary politics a seduction, a simulacra, where citizens get only spectacle because that's all they want. American political critic Wilson Carey McWilliams has a similar concern about the visual aspects of politics, but for a different reason: he believes we lose our commitments and sense of community when we base decisions on the visual, our most superficial sense. That belief parallels Postman's. Even stronger language comes from John Welsh, who sees us living in a political world of government by mystification. Because we are constantly, in his words, confronted by "the dramatization of authority," we end up being submerged in the "dramaturgical technology of the American state," where the people lose all ability to control the system.

These are important concerns, though, as I've suggested, to put all of the blame for the bad parts of American politics on visualization is to search for a scapegoat too easy to pick out of the herd. While questions of authority and spectacle must be approached seriously, I want to raise what I take to be an even more fundamental question: the question of moral character and political decision making.

As I noted earlier, I think the combination of words, sounds, and visual images that comprise today's electric political rhetoric allow us to explore political character more seriously than ever. And that is all to the good. But yet, I think it is accompanied by a danger: that citizens of the United States will make *all* of their political decisions—especially their voting decisions—on their assessment of character. While even Aristotle recognized that arguments over character were the most important arguments an advocate could make, he never suggested we rely solely on characterological arguments when exercising our political judgment.

I believe that most voters feel so overwhelmed by issues that are far too complicated for them to understand that they finally throw up their hands, say take my tax money but don't hurt me, and then hope they've elected someone with enough human decency and with a large enough vision to do some good for the country. In a complicated world, in other words, the natural tendency is to retreat to character—to hope that good, moral folks will be able to guide us through the complexities of the late-modern, perhaps even postmodern, world.

The problem with such a feeling, of course, is that reigns of virtue have seldom succeeded. While I suppose you could argue that Charlemagne's Holy Roman Empire operated successfully, for a while, as a virtuous community, the fact remains that few have made a go of it. Oliver Cromwell's Protestant protectorate in England lasted less than twenty years; the New England theocracies crashed under the weight of their arbitrary rules for living; the Reign of Virtue in revolutionary France turned into a reign of terror; Communism's classless society produced Stalin's death camps and the crushing of ethnic revolts in Hungary and Czechoslovakia; in the contemporary Yugoslavian republics, the search for religious social freedom has turned into an absolute intolerance of those who are ethnically different. Hitler, Mussolini, Amin, and far too many other fascist leaders have created cults of personality—cults of character—that lead to prejudice, discrimination, and death. And, I would add, that similar problems occur on a smaller scale, as when a state or even a county votes in leadership on the basis of perceived virtue.

I am not suggesting, of course, that we need leaders without moral convictions. Of course we need them. Rather, the point is that we cannot select leaders solely or, perhaps, even primarily because of their public character. Electric political rhetoric tends to emphasize characters as they play out their politics in sociodramas. We must be able to punch through those dramas; we must be able to penetrate the portrayals of character, so as to raise questions about real problems that are faced by real people. When the state of Iowa was flooding out in the summer of 1993, we were helped less by the Washington debate over how disaster relief should be paid for than by the men and women who drove tanker trucks of clean water up from northern Missouri for use by the citizens of Des Moines. Unless we realize that action includes more than getting an appearance on *Larry King Live* or *Issues and Answers,* and unless professions of virtue translate into concrete political acts in local communities, our political system will continue to be characterized by gridlock. As citizens, we need to value *logos,* the reasoned bases of action, as much as *ethos,* the characterological part. And, more than that, we need to force politicians to put their money and programs where their mouths are.

And I'm convinced that can happen. Like many observers of the political scene, I came out of the 1988 election depressed. It was one of the nastiest electoral wars ever waged in this country, only 50.1 percent of our eligible electorate bothered to vote, and the public was utterly disgusted. But then came 1992. It certainly wasn't an ideal contest, I suppose, but at least the people, the citizens, seized a lot of initiatives, pushing for more non-candidate controlled television appearances, using hotlines and newspaper "truth boxes" to ask for information and demand the facts, and to scare the major parties with their support of H. Ross Perot. Our voter turnout reversed the long decline it's been in since 1960, and political optimism increased. Hope was in the air.

Whether that hope will be rewarded remains to be seen. But, I am optimistic. As John Dewey noted over seventy-five years ago, "Communication is a process of sharing experience till it becomes a common possession." And, I'm convinced that in the electronic age we have far more tools of communication than ever before, and hence a far, far greater chance of making experience a common possession than ever before. What we need to do, therefore, is not to condemn the electric rhetoric that sparks into our homes through either the television or cable, but to study it, to understand it, and ultimately to make it work for the public good.

If I may quote William Norwood Brigance one more time, "People's modes of thinking develop out of their way of life." Just so for you: your way of thinking, for better or worse, has grown out of your experience in the era of electric life. That era has revolutionized even for what counts as politics, and now it is time you seize the day and put your knowledge of electric life to work for you in political dens from Crawfordsville, Indiana, to the District of Columbia, wish you marvelous good luck in making your citizen's role a significant one. That would make William Norwood Brigance very proud.

# THE AFRICAN AMERICAN EXPERIENCE

## LINCOLN, LABOR, AND THE BLACK MILITARY: THE LEGACY PROVIDED[1]
### William B. Gould IV[2]

In 1976 the United States government first officially recognized Black History Month. In reality, the event dated back to 1926 when the historian Carter G. Woodson selected February to honor the achievements of African Americans because it was the month in which both Abraham Lincoln and Frederick Douglass were born.

Among the many events during Black History Month in 1995 was a speech by William B. Gould IV to the Military Order of the Loyal Legion of the United States on the subjects of Lincoln, labor, and the history of African Americans in the military, including Gould's great-grandfather, grandfather, and father. Mr. Gould was the first African-American chairman of the National Labor Relations Board and the Charles A. Beardsley Professor of Law at Stanford University. Appropriately, the speech was given on February 11, the eve of Abraham Lincoln's birthday.

In the speech, Gould analyzed President Lincoln's legacy on the development of democratic institutions and the protection of human rights in the United States. More specifically, Gould dwelt on Lincoln's views on labor and the right to strike as well as his efforts to incorporate African Americans into the armed forces.

The speech was considered to be significant enough that both Senator Carol Moseley Braun and Representative Anna G. Eshoo inserted it into the *Congressional Record*.

*Mr. Gould's speech:* "I heard the glad tidings that the Stars and Stripes have been planted over the Capitol of the Confederacy by the invincible Grant. While we honor the living soldiers who have done so much we must not forget to whisper for fear of disturbing the glorious sleep of the men who have fallen. Martyrs to

---

[1]Delivered to the Military Order of the Loyal Legion of the United States on February 11, 1995.

[2]For biographical note see Appendix.

the cause of Right and Equality"—Diary of William B. Gould,
April 15, 1865.

These are the words of my great-grandfather written 130
years ago at the time of Appomattox. They reflect the thoughts
and passion of one of our country's black naval veterans of the
Civil War and his commitment to the military initiatives waged by
President Lincoln.

It is meet and right that we come here this evening to honor
the memory of Abraham Lincoln, the sixteenth President of the
United States, properly known throughout the world as the Great
Emancipator. The New World's central political and social
achievement, the Emancipation Proclamation which President
Lincoln authored, transcends the ages and future generations.
And his ideas about democracy and the rights of all people consti-
tute the central vision of the American democratic system today.

As the sons of Union officers who fought in the Civil War, you
know better than most that this 186th anniversary of Lincoln's
birthday marks anew the ongoing struggle to free our country
from the legacy of the odious institution of slavery so that all
people may live out their lives and fulfill their aspirations without
the actuality or fear of arbitrary limitation.

One of my law professors used to say that the "greatest constitutional decision ever rendered occurred when Pickett's charge
failed at Gettysburg." The legacy of Appomattox and all that led
to it resonates throughout our society to this evening here in
Washington as part of the unceasing struggle against all arbitrary
barriers which afflict mankind.

And both Gettysburg and Appomattox produced the great
Civil War amendments to the Constitution, which reversed the
infamous *Dred Scott* decision in which the Supreme Court declared blacks to be property constitutionally. The amendments, in
turn, have provided our country with the historical framework
for both the Supreme Court's great *Brown v Board of Education*,
1954 ruling condemning separate but equal as a denial of equal
protection and also the modern civil rights movement as well as
the legislation that it produced. Similarly, Title VII of the Civil
Rights Act of 1964, our most comprehensive anti-discrimination
legislation relating to the workplace, is a lineal descendant of the
previous century's developments.

I am not a Lincoln or Civil War scholar. Indeed, I find the
amount of literature about both subjects to be daunting—and,
accordingly, I know that you do not expect a scholarly examina-

tion of President Lincoln from me. But there are matters which have and do involve me both practically and professionally with Lincoln and his times.

The first is that I am the fourteenth Chairman of the National Labor Relations Board and, as such, administer an agency and interpret a statute which both seek to implement some of Lincoln's most basic views on labor.

The second is that I am the great-grandson of the first William Benjamin Gould who, along with seven other "contraband" (seized property—the appellation which General Benjamin Butler gave to escaped slaves) set sail in a small boat from Cape Fear, North Carolina and boarded the *USS Cambridge* on September 22, 1862, the day that President Lincoln announced his intent to issue the Emancipation Proclamation. You will know that the Proclamation states in relevant part:

> "And I further declare and make known, that such persons of suitable condition [the freed slaves held by those in rebellion], will be received into the armed service of the United States to garrison forts, positions, stations, and other places, and to man vessels of all sorts in said service."

And thus it was that William B. Gould joined the United States Navy and served as landsman and steward on the North Atlantic Blockade and subsequently served on vessels visiting Britain, France, Belgium, Portugal and Spain, chasing the Confederate ships which were built by their undercover allies.

In 1864 the American Minister Charles Francis Adams had notified the British government that if the *Alabama* and the *Georgia*—two iron clad "rams" built by the British for the Confederacy—were allowed to go to sea, this would be construed by the United States as a declaration of war. William B. Gould sailed with the steam frigate *Niagara* for the European station to join other vessels such as the *Kearsarge* to keep, in my great-grandfather's words, a "sharp lookout" for these vessels. The *Niagara's* destination was the Bay of Biscay where she eventually engaged in battle.

William B. Gould's service ended on September 29, 1865 when he made the following entry in his diary:

> "At the Navy Yard [Charlestown, Massachusetts] at five o'clock I received my discharge being three years and nine days in the service of Uncle Samuel and glad am I to receive it . . . [pay] of four hundred and twenty four dollars. So end my service in the Navy of the United States of America."

I did not know the first William B. Gould for he died—in

Dedham, Massachusetts where he resided from 1871 onward—thirteen years before my birth. I did not know my grandfather, William B. Gould, Jr., a Spanish-American War veteran, for he was to die nine years later in 1932. But the third William B. Gould was my greatest inspiration in my most formative years—and my belief is that the values and culture which he attempted to transmit to me were very much a part of the lives of the first two gentlemen to whom I have referred.

Truly then, President Lincoln's views and policies have had a major impact upon my own life.

As Chairman of the National Labor Relations Board, I have a responsibility to implement a statute which promotes the right of employees to band together for the purpose of protecting or improving their own working conditions, to join unions, to engage in collective bargaining and to be free from various forms of discrimination. This statute, enacted as part of President Franklin D. Roosevelt's New Deal in 1935, is one of the country's proudest achievements, expressing the policy that the protection of "the exercise by workers of full freedom of association, self-organization, and designation of representatives of their own choosing, for the purpose of negotiating the terms and conditions of their employment or other mutual aid or protection" should be encouraged.

In recent years, a number of scholars and critics, like myself, took note of the fact that the statute has not been working well in implementing these objectives because of poor administrative processes and ineffective remedies. Some of these matters can be and are being cured by us at the Board and some can be only addressed by Congress. I hope to do what I can to make continued progress in the former category before I depart from Washington and return to California a few years down the road when my term ends.

I enthusiastically support the views contained in the preamble and have made my position known in books, articles, and speeches. In many respects, the fundamentally similar views of President Lincoln were a precursor of our own 1935 legislation.

Recall what Lincoln said to the New York Workingmen's Democratic Republican Association on March 21, 1864:

"The strongest bond of human sympathy, outside of the family relation, should be one uniting all working people, of all nations, and tongues and kindreds."

As the Presidential campaign of 1860 unfolded, Lincoln stated his philosophy in these terms:

"When one starts poor, as most do in the race of life, free society is such that he knows he can better his condition; he knows that there is no fixed condition of labor for his whole life. I want every man to have the chance—and I believe a black man is entitled to it—in which he can better his condition—when he may look forward and hope to be a hired laborer this year and the next, work for himself afterward, and finally to hire men to work for him! That is the true system."

In the same speech, Lincoln makes clear that the right to strike is integral to a democratic society, a policy reflected in the language of Sections 7 and 13 of the National Labor Relations Act and in the Norris-LaGuardia Act of 1932 which preceded it. Just a few weeks ago, President Clinton took note of one of our law's limitations in his statement criticizing the Bridgestons/Firestone Company's use of permanent striker replacements, noting that such tactics show the need to enact legislation prohibiting such a denial of the fundamental right to strike.

It bears note that Lincoln's view of labor and the right to strike ran against the tide of laissez-faire thinking which predominated in the previous century—thinking which has reared its head again toward the close of this century, one of its forms being the repressive striker replacement weapon of which President Clinton spoke. President Lincoln supported the right to strike and spoke out in the spring of 1860 in support of a well-organized strike conducted by the boot and shoe workers in New England. Lincoln regarded the right to strike by free labor as a "virtue, not a failing, of free society," as G. S. Boritt has written in "Lincoln and the Economics of the American Dream."

Boritt also notes that during the Civil War several delegations of strikers from the Machinists and Blacksmiths Union of New York visited the White House and spoke to the President about their position. States Boritt:

"The labor representatives took great comfort from their interview, reasoning that although their employers refused to deal with them, Lincoln received them. 'If any man should again say that combinations of working men are not good,' they concluded, 'let them point to the Chief Magistrate.' They even quoted the President as saying 'I know that in almost every case of strikes, the men have just cause for complaint.' It is rather likely that the union men quoted Lincoln correctly."

Of course, Lincoln's view of labor was closely related to his view of slavery. Again, in 1860 he said: "'Owned labor' wouldcompete with free labor so as to 'degrade' the latter." And, in an earlier and lengthy speech to the Wisconsin State Agricultural Society in Milwaukee on September 30, 1859, he noted that the so-called "mud-sill" theory was that a hired laborer is "fatally fixed in that condition for life" and thus his condition is the same as that of a slave.

But as Lincoln noted, this theory proceeded upon the assumption that labor and education were incompatible and that one could not improve oneself and one's family through free labor. Lincoln's view was antithetical to all of this. He held the view that workers should be able to rise to new horizons.

And this view is closely related to another held by the President which has similar contemporary implications. Because Lincoln believed that all people could improve themselves and thus rise out of their station if opportunity were afforded them, unlike other proponents of the rights of labor, he did not see the working class as a well-defined unit, notwithstanding his endorsement of its use of the strike to defend its interests and act jointly in its dealings with employers. To some extent, said Professor Boritt, Lincoln shared the view that there was a harmony between the capital and labor and that it ought to be promoted so as to enhance the ability of workers to rise out of their class.

Again, these views resonate with us today as Congress considers proposals to enhance employee participation and proposed amendments to the National Labor Relations Act which will achieve this goal. I believe that President Lincoln would be sympathetic with contemporary efforts to promote employee involvement in the workplace and thus enhance our industry's global competitiveness—so long as such reforms do not interfere with the ability of the workers and unions to defend their own positions, a proposition that I have long advanced.

The view that an individual was not "fatally fixed" in a particular condition forever constitutes the philosophy which prevailed in the Civil War and through the Emancipation Proclamation and the enactment of the Thirteenth Amendment which Lincoln sponsored before his assassination. Again, this is reflected anew in last month's State of the Union address by President Clinton when, in advocating new minimum wage legislation, he said that the worker who works must have his "reward" and that the job of government is to "expand opportunity to empower people to make the most of their own lives."

This is what is at the heart of modern democracy and the Bill of Rights for workers in the private sector which are continued in the National Labor Relations Act and similar statutes. And this has been the assumption behind the struggle for equality which has attempted to make good on the promise of emancipation in the previous century.

My great-grandfather, a mason who worked with his mind and hands and established a business as a contractor, employing other workers in Dedham, Massachusetts, benefited from the above-noted philosophy and the quoted portions of the Emancipation Proclamation. Said William B. Gould on March 8, 1863, two months after its issuance:

"Read the Proclamation of Emancipation very [sic] good."

The policy, of course, had evolved in fits and starts. As Benjamin Quarles has noted in "The Negro in the Civil War," General Butler was the first to devise a policy of acceptance of blacks who wanted to fight with the North. This was, as Quarles noted, the most "insistent" problem faced by the Lincoln Administration in 1861 and 1862. It emerged, as he has noted, after the Union defeat at Bull Run which was attributable "in part to the Confederate military defenses constructed by slaves."

Congress enacted legislation which provided for the forfeiture of all slaves whose masters had permitted them to be used in the military or naval service of the Confederacy. Quarles notes that the 1861 legislation "strengthened the hand of the small band of Union officers from the beginning had been in favor of freeing the slaves." Two military initiatives—one designed by John C. Fremont in July 1861, "The Pathfinder," and the other undertaken by Major General Dave Hunter in the summer of 1862—were both rescinded by Lincoln out of his concern with preserving the allegiance of the border states.

The Confiscation Act enacted on July 17, 1862, declaring free all slaves who were owned by those in rebellion was the next step in the process. This had the effect of increasing the number of fugitives in whom the United States Navy expressed a particular interest so as to make use of the information that they could provide about enemy locations and movements. As summer became fall the problem became more "insistent."

Three days after my great-grandfather boarded the *USS Cambridge* came this report of Commander G.H. Scott regarding the blockage of Wilmington

"Fourteen contrabands have reached the 'Monticello' and 'Penobscot' and several the 'Cambridge' within a few days, and as the vessels have not room for them, will you please direct what disposition shall be made of them?"

We know what disposition was made of William B. Gould. On October 3, 1862, he said

"All of us shipped today for three years, first taking the Oath of Allegiance to the government of Uncle Samuel."

Thus he, and eventually I, benefited from both the Confiscation Act and the new policy expressed in the Emancipation Proclamation which was not to be effective for another three months. His service was made possible because of it. This was then his opportunity—and his observations, hopes and views are chronicled in the diary which he kept between 1862 and 1865.

On the perils of the seas and their storminess, he says:

"[T]he gale still blows fresh and the seas running verry [sic] high. We shipped several through the night and one—fill'd the Ward Room with Water I have got ducked awfully last night. It was worth something to be upon the Deck. Although there is much danger in a storm there is something very sublime to hear the roar of the storm. The hissing of the Waves, the whistling of the Rigging and the Cannon like report of the torn sail and above all the stern word of the commander and the—sound of the boatswain's pipe all adds to the grandeur of the scene. For there is something grand in a storm. Allnight with eager eyes both Officers and Men paced the deck watching our Foretopsail, feeling in a measure secure as long as we could sail at all. It has it stood through the night. There was no sign of the storm abateing [sic]. All the galley fire is out and nothing to eat is the cry and almost nothing to wear on account of the Water. Shine out fair sun and smote the Waves that we may proceed on our course and all be saved."

And on December 25 and December 27 of 1862, he had this to say about the loneliness of his work off New Inlet:

"This being Christmas I think of the table at home cruised around as usual. Fine weather but very lonesome in the absence of news and we all had the Blues."

While on the North Atlantic Blockade with the *USS Cambridge* he says on November 17, 1862:

"A sail was reported close under the land right ahead. We gave chase. When within range of our boat we told them good morning in the shape of a shot for her to heave to."

But then he describes the difficulties that arose:

"To this [the shot] they took no notice. We sent another which fell under her stern the ship stood for the Beach. Shot after shot was set after her but they heeded not we immediately manned the first cutter and sent her to board and destroy her. We also sent two other boats to lend assistance [after sending a line to these boats so that they could return to the main ship] they got the Boat all ready to come out when a body of Rebel Soldiers dashed over the hill at the double quick and all were prisoners. We could see them from the ship marching off our men and dragging the boats after them. We lost eleven men and three officers. Rather a bad day's work."

But the fortunes of war were not all negative as testified to by him in this entry in the summer of 1864 off Portugal:

"[W]e made a steamer and stood for her. She kept on her course without any until we got within 5 miles of her when she suddenly changed her course. We beat to Quarters and Fired a shot. She showed the English collors [sic]. We Fired another. When she came to be boarded her and found her to be the Rebel Privateer 'Georgia' from Liverpool on her way to refit a cruiser. But the next cruise that she makes will be for Uncle Samuel . . . this capture makes a crew feel very [sic] proud."

While in the English Channel:

"[W]e took on board an English Pilot who brought the thrice glorious news of the sinking of the 'Alabama' by 'Kearsarge' off Cherbough . . . [A]lthough we have been disappointment to us in not getting a shot at the 'Alabama' we are satisfied that she is out of the way."

And in 1864 while serving on the *Niagara* he said about the people that he saw in Spain:

"[I]t looks very strange in this country which nature have lavished with riches that there should be so many poor people."

And again on the shameful treatment of black soldiers on his ship:

"Yesterday about 900 men of the Maryland (colored) regiment came on board (they being transfered to the Navy) and took dinner then departed for Portsmouth, New Hampshire. They were treated very rough by the crew. They refused to let them eat out of the mess pans and call them all kinds of names. One man (had) his watch stolen from him by these scoundrels. In all they were treated shamefully."

On the proposed colonization of blacks to Africa or the Caribbean:

"We see by the papers that President (Johnson) intimates colonization for the colored people of the United States. This move of his must and shall be resisted. We were born under the Flag of the union and never will we know no other. My sentiment is the sentiment of the people of the States."

All of this ended in 1865 and provided William B. Gould with his chance at life. Sometimes I think about his thoughts as he walked the streets of Wilmington a young man and what would have been had he stayed in North Carolina and the events of those four critical years had not taken place. Most certainly his great-grandson would not be here today addressing you as Chairman of the National Labor Relations Board.

I am privileged to have this opportunity in 1995 to contribute to the public good in the most inspirational and progressive Administration in Washington since the 1960s—one which is unabashedly committed to the principles of those who fell 130 years ago.

My hope is that I can reflect well upon the first William B. Gould and the chance that he made for me by rising out of his "fixed station," to use Lincoln's words, and I am all too aware of the limitations of time as we move rapidly toward a new millennium.

As William B. Gould said on December 31, 1863, in New York harbor:

> "We are obliged knock off on the account of the storm. It blew very hard from South East. The old year of '1863' went out furiously as if it was angry with all the world because it had finished the time allotted to it. Sooner or later we must follow."

My first major impression during my first trip outside of the United States in 1962, as a student at the London School of Economics, is of the grand and majestic statue of President Lincoln which sits in Parliament Square today. Now I live in Washington within a mile of the great Lincoln Memorial in which his brooding historical omnipresence is made so manifest.

You and I, the entire nation and the world honor President Lincoln and his policies tonight. Both personally and professionally they are with me always as is the legacy provided by him and so many others in what my great-grandfather called:

"[T]he holiest of all causes, Liberty and Union."

---

## THE STRUGGLE IS NOT OVER[1]
### Vernon E. Jordan, Jr.[2]

---

At one time speakers at college and university commencement exercises were expected to deliver addresses whose main purpose was to inspire the graduates to go out to improve the world. In recent years, however, at many commencement exercises speakers have used the occasion to discuss important nation-

[1]Delivered at the commencement exercises at North Carolina Central University in Durham, North Carolina on May 14, 1994.
[2]For biographical note see Appendix.

al and world problems and present their views on the problems. Vernon E. Jordan, Jr., chose both the earlier and more modern formats: he inspired his listeners and called their attention to what he felt was a significant need.

Jordan delivered his address at the predominantly African-American North Carolina Central University commencement in Durham, North Carolina, on May 14, 1994. An activist and leader in the American civil rights movement, Jordan later served as president of the National Urban League for many years. Regarded as one of the most eloquent speakers in the country, Jordan currently is a senior partner in the law firm of Akin, Gump, Strauss, Hauer & Feld.

Early in his address, Jordan stated his theme that ideas have the power to influence far away events. The event he had in mind occurred that month ten thousand miles away in South Africa where Nelson Mandela had been elected as its first black president after spending twenty-seven years in jail because of his opposition to apartheid. Jordan attributed the end of segregation in South Africa and the election of Mandela to the power of ideas.

Then comparing the United States to South Africa, Jordan urged the graduating students and others in the audience to commit themselves to continue the fight for equality for African Americans, citing specific goals and problems to be addressed.

*Mr. Jordan's speech:* It has been said that commencement speakers have a lot in common with grandfather clocks. Both are over six feet tall, ponderous in construction, more traditional than functional, and noisily communicate commonplace information. I shared that view until I started giving commencement addresses. It's amazing how different things seem from this side of the podium.

My own commencement featured a speaker whose name no one remembers, a message no one understood, and a speech that confused longevity with immortality. Don't worry, my words will be fewer and my message is relevant to you, something close to home. But before coming close to home, let's go far away—ten thousand miles away, to a new South Africa.

This month, Nelson Mandela was elected president of a free, reborn South Africa. It was once a land where the black majority was deprived of basic human rights, a land where black people were denied the vote, a land where freedom fighters were driven into prison and exile.

Today, South Africa, the land of apartheid, is a free nation with a black president, Nelson Mandela, who emerged from 27 years of prison without bitterness, without hate, and with a mission to reconcile all South Africans. When Nelson Mandela was once asked how he survived 27 years in prison, he answered that he spent his life in prison before being formally jailed.

Today, South Africa's white minority is fearful, wondering whether it has a future in a multi-racial nation. It should look to the American South, whose white people were liberated by the civil rights movement as much as its black people were. Once the system of segregation was destroyed, the south rejoined the nation. Its economy flourished. Freedom came for whites as well as Blacks. Now people of both races can speak freely, think freely, act freely.

So the brave march to freedom of Nelson Mandela and South Africa's black people will secure freedom for white South Africans, just as the civil rights movement freed white southerners. That became clear to me when I went to South Africa on a fact-finding mission in 1976. When I was clearing customs, the officer asked an incredible question. He didn't ask if I was carrying guns. He didn't ask if I was carrying bombs. He didn't ask if I was carrying drugs. He asked if I was carrying books! Mind control!

In a way, he was right, because guns, bombs and drugs do not endanger a police state, ideas do. Apartheid was overthrown by the idea of democracy.

Racial supremacy was overthrown by the idea of a multi-racial nation. Such is the power of ideas.

Victor Hugo was right: "Greater than the tread of mighty armies is an idea whose time has come."

Today in America, we too must assert the power of ideas. We must assert the power of our democratic ideas so that all of our people have the tools with which to become informed, active citizens participating in the civic life of the nation.

And we must assert the idea of equal opportunity so that all of our people have the education and the skills to become productive, active citizens participating in the economic life of our nation.

Those ideas must be put into practice in every state, city, and township in America. Colleges and universities, community organizations, business and labor, and political leaders must work together to implement those ideas.

And that holds true on the national level. In many ways the

Clinton Administration is setting an example for local governments and for the private sector. For the first time in over a dozen years, we now have leadership in Washington that is committed to helping to build an open, pluralistic, integrated society. It has reached out to Blacks, Hispanics, Jews, women, gays, and other groups to construct an administration that looks like the nation it leads.

It has taken on the really tough problems that face us all, problems like health care, welfare, education, crime, and jobs.

And President Clinton has not only talked of the need for people to have opportunities. He has talked of the need for people to accept responsibilities. That is of special importance to black Americans. For as Frederick Douglass said, "Men may not get all they pay for in this world, but they must certainly pay for all they get."

In the context of today's world, that means we cannot expect crime-free communities without working to restore the values and attitudes that helped us overcome the bitter past. It means we cannot expect to achieve equal opportunities unless we work to get the training and skills that qualify us for those opportunities. It means we cannot expect young people to succeed in the world of the 21st century unless we nurture healthy family life and help them develop into proud, productive citizens. It means we have to look to the White House, the State House, and City Hall for policies that create opportunities. But at the same time, we have to fight for those policies, we have to be involved in the electoral process, we have to educate ourselves about the issues and vote to advance our strategic interests.

And we must also look to ourselves, and mobilize our own communities to deal with those problems only we can deal with.

Frederick Douglass' timeless words also carry a special message for black college graduates.

We who have had the fortune to achieve a level of education that opens doors of opportunities must not only seize those opportunities we must work to assure that our less fortunate brothers and sisters get them too. Your degree is a mandate to rise to a higher level of maturity about yourselves, your world, and your responsibilities.

It is written in Corinthians, "When I was a child, I spoke as a child, I understood as a child, I thought as a child; but when I became a man, I put away childish things."

You are now men and women with college degrees. You are

now among the elite minority of college-educated black people. You now face a future of options and possibilities unknown to most black people.

My question to you, graduates, is what will you do with your degree, with your responsibilities, with your lives? I ask that question in a spirit of deep concern for the future.

For the masses of black people today are mired in poverty, imprisoned in urban and rural ghettos, caught in the crossfire of violence, crime, drugs, poor education, and a lack of marketable skills.

If we as a people are to climb out of that abyss, if we are to take our proud and rightful place in this nation, those wrongs must be righted, those deficits must be corrected.

And it is you, and young people like you, who must take the lead in that noble cause.

Are you prepared for that responsibility?

I ask the question because I followed with interest the extraordinary "Freak-nik" during spring break, when some 200,000 black college students went to Atlanta for a long weekend of partying and merrymaking. They spent some $20 million that weekend, according to press reports.

I was proud of those young people because from all accounts they acted responsibly. Given the numbers, there were very few incidents that might be deplored.

But I was a little disappointed too. I wonder how $20 million was spent by students, most of whom receive financial aid packages from their schools. I wonder how much of that $20 million spent that weekend found its way into the hands of black businesses and black workers in Atlanta. I wonder about the seriousness of our best and brightest young people, when, with 200,000 in one place, there were no organized cultural and educational events for them to join.

No plays or concerts planned, no lectures given, no papers presented, no seminars organized to discuss the great issues of our time.

I wonder why there were no organized meetings with black businesspeople, no sessions planned to tutor black kids, no efforts made to register black voters.

And I wonder, too, how many of the bull sessions that weekend were about how America can end poverty, how to improve race relations, how to rebuild black family life.

I understand the need to blow off some steam. And I love

partying too. But I still wonder at the appropriateness of a "Freak-nik" that had no room for experiences beyond partying.

I thought back to a time 30 years ago when other students went south. They left their campuses to soldier in a vast army that challenged the system of segregation. They risked their lives to register black people in the hinterlands of Mississippi and the rural places of Alabama. They risked hosings and beatings to march for justice in the meanest towns of the south. They put themselves in the way of danger to bring hope to the poorest and most neglected among us. Because of those young people, the south changed and the nation changed.

Those students of the 1960s, your mothers and fathers, were in the grip of a powerful idea, the idea of equality, whose time they hastened and whose force overcame the tread of mighty armies of racism and segregation. And they took that maturing experience to become pioneers themselves, blazing trails in corporate America, in government, and in the professions.

You may think that's ancient history, events that happened before you were born. But the struggle is not over. Yesterday's students began something that today's young people must finish.

For despite the tremendous gains that have taken place over the past three decades, too much, far too much, remains the same.

Discrimination still flourishes, although it is now illegal. Poverty still flourishes, and while there is less of it than in the past, in many ways it is more concentrated and more devastating. The vision of an open, pluralistic, integrated society is still a distant vision. In large part, that is because white society has been reluctant to abandon the artificial distinctions of race. But we must also admit that some of us prefer to retreat into a self-imposed apartheid, unwilling to risk full participation in the broader society.

So there was plenty of room for a serious side to the "Freak-nik"; room for a teach-in about the realities of life for black people in America today, room for culture and serious thinking along with the partying.

For the situation of black people today is such that we cannot afford to squander our energies and our resources in the pursuit of fun. We must invest them in the pursuit of knowledge and action. And we must invest them in serious thinking about our personal futures and the future of all black people. And the burden of doing that thinking and acting falls heaviest on those best able to do it, you, our new college graduates.

For I must again ask, "What will you do with your degree, with your responsibilities, with your lives?"

You are entering a very difficult environment. Our world often seems a confused and hard place. The changing economy means competition for good jobs will be fierce, and the penalties for failure even fiercer.

But you enter this often cold world with the education and the college degree that are entrance tickets to success for those who are willing to work hard and to excel. You must be conscious of the fact that many of you have advantages that your parents never had; advantages that some other brothers and sisters do not have. Your horizons are wider; your prospects better.

Whatever the future holds for you, must acknowledge a responsibility to the black community. You must enter into the serious work of helping black people survive and thrive in the 21st century. You must strengthen our community institutions to meet the great challenges ahead, institutions that have nurtured black hopes and aspirations through long years of oppression and neglect.

Among those institutions are the predominately black colleges and universities. They will rise or fall on your active involvement and on your generosity in raising and giving the funds to educate future generations. This is a grave responsibility. You cannot take your degree and run. You, who have benefited from the sacrifices of the past must return something to the future.

Black colleges, whether public or private, cannot continue to go to white philanthropists or state legislatures for support if their own graduates fail to honor their obligation to support their alma mater.

The degree you are receiving today is an admission ticket to a better life. For most of you, this university has provided the financial aid that allowed you to get a college education.

Nothing in this world is for free. You have a moral debt to pay, a responsibility to help others get ahead, too.

By doing so, you will demonstrate real black power. For real black power is the creative use of green power to support black institutions, black colleges, and black community organizations so they can be strong, vital pillars of a strong, vital community.

I am confident that you will succeed in your lives, in your careers, and in meeting your obligations to the community. I am confident that as you hear the anguished cry of our people asking, pleading, "Is there no balm in Gilead? Is there no physician there?" Armed with your degree and training, I am confident you will turn the question mark into an exclamation point, answering, "Yes, there is a balm in Gilead. There is a physician there to heal the body and soul of our people."

So as you depart these hallowed grounds of central, as you bid farewell to your alma mater, remember: you have a charge to keep, a calling to fulfill, a rendezvous with destiny. And as you go forth, may you mount up with wings as eagles, may you run and not be weary, may you walk together children and not be faint.

## DEFINING AMERICAN FOREIGN POLICY[1]
### GEORGE F. KENNAN[2]

To honor George F. Kennan's contributions to the country as a statesman and scholar of American foreign policy, friends and admirers established the George F. Kennan Award for Distinguished Public Service. The first award was made on October 17, 1994, at a ceremony at the Waldorf-Astoria Hotel in New York City.

When organizers of the award asked Ambassador Kennan to deliver an address at the ceremony, he at first declined for reasons of age and health. Subsequently, persuaded that many of the founders and supporters of the award wanted to hear his view of what should constitute the general thrust of American foreign policy in the post Cold-War era, he agreed to do so.

Senator Claibourne Pell, who inserted Ambassador Kennan's remarks in the *Congressional Record* (December 1, 1994, S 15401), expressed admiration for Kennan and his speech and commented:

Ambassador Kennan, a self-described man of this century—and, I would add, one of the century's most visionary statesmen—offers some perspectives on the 100 years. I was particularly struck by the fact that Ambassador Kennan, who defined the overriding theme of the cold war period—containment—does not believe a central policy thrust is definable at this time. He says, "What we need is not any single policy. That would be quite impossible at this point. What we need is a variety of policies."

*Ambassador Kennan's speech:* Mr. Flynn, Doctor Schwab, ladies and gentlemen: I think you will all know without my laboring the point how deeply I appreciate this honor. I feel very inadequate to know how to acknowledge it. It would be difficult for anyone, I think to respond to the honor itself and to the lovely things that have just been said. If the task of this committee is, as I have always assumed it to be, to promote sound and constructive thinking about the problems of American foreign policy, then the conferring of this

---

[1]Delivered at the ceremony of the first George F. Kennan Award for Distinguished Public Service at the Waldorf Astoria Hotel in New York City on October 17, 1994.

[2]For biographical note see Appendix.

award enables me to think that my own efforts of these past years have been at least supplementary to those of the committee, and that in itself gives me deep satisfaction and encouragement.

When Dr. Schwab first spoke to me last spring about the possibility of such an occasion, I told him that honored as I would be, of course, by the award, I could not, for reasons of age and health, contemplate giving an address. This remains, for better or for worse, the situation, but I have been told recently that there were expectations in one quarter or another that I would say something about my view of what should constitute the general thrust of American foreign policy in this post cold war era, and this I will try to do, although necessarily very briefly.

I must say, before I begin my remarks, that this is a very intimidating group of people I have before me. I see a great many people who know a lot more than I do about the things I'll be talking about, and I feel a certain hesitation in saying anything at all about our policy of the present day. I am, after all, a man of this past century, and what we are getting into now is the century that is about to dawn on us. At times, I thought I knew something about the century that will soon pass; but I'm sure that I do not know nor can I foresee a great deal about the century that is coming. Nevertheless, I will say a few words.

If the suggestion is that I outline a central thrust of American foreign policy to replace that which preoccupied us during the period of the Cold War, then I can say only that this is a very difficult thing for me to respond to. I don't think there is any central thrust of policy possible at this time. It is a varied, very confused, very unbalanced, and uncertain world that we face. What we need is not any single policy. That would be quite impossible at this point. What we need is a variety of policies. But perhaps there is one unifying factor that could bring these things together, and that is the question of motivation, of purpose, and what we conceive ourselves to be doing. This question, I think, can take two forms: One is a very natural traditional and unavoidable concern for our military and political security and for the security of our closest allies. The other is the hope, endemic, I think, to all generations of Americans, that we, as a great democratic people, will be able to play a useful and effective role in promoting peace, stability, and humane government in other parts of the world.

In the years since communism broke down, our military security, providentially, has not been seriously threatened. That is true for most though not all of our allies. So perhaps it was only

natural that we should have concentrated a large part of our
attention on and invested a large part of our efforts in being
helpful to others in troubled situations involving, for the most
part, countries other than those in the advanced areas of Europe
and the Far East. I have in mind, of course, such places as Korea,
Iraq, the Balkans, the Near East, Somalia, and now Haiti.

I have few criticisms to make of the way in which we have
handled these situations. I have only admiration and pride for
the way in which our armed forces have conducted themselves in
performing the tasks to which they have been assigned, tasks that,
in many instances, were quite the limits of their traditional training. I think that they have been models of what military people
can do in difficult circumstances.

With the exception of Somalia and the still unfinished intervention in Haiti, I do not see that our government had any choice
but to respond to those situations in the way that it did. And,
finally, after all the political wrangling and jousting and mutual
denunciations about foreign policy that have gone on here at
home, I consider that both administrations, that of Mr. Bush and
that of Mr. Clinton, have handled these various situations diplo-
matically in a reasonably sound and creditable manner. I hope
that, when these involvements have been liquidated in a way that
is consistent with the preservation of the honor and dignity of this
country (and, in this instance, that is going to be, I am afraid, a
very long time), we will not be in too much of a hurry to replace
those involvements with others.

All that being said, I still have some anxieties to voice about various
ventures. But, first, I must say (and some of you may find this hard to
believe) that I have anxieties about the highly dangerous and urgent
problems, social, political, and economic, that we have right here in
our own country. They are problems that the media have found it
hard to recognize and that the politicians have found it hard to
admit but I hope that these problems will soon become the subject of
national debate, that they will receive the attention and the discussion that they deserve, and for this it is desirable that we be not too
distracted with the involvements and problems beyond our borders.

Second, we have our relations with the other great powers, and
we must not permit our preoccupations with the less developed
world to distract us from doing justice to the importance of those
relations. We have before us in this respect a situation, a providential
situation, I think, namely, that for the first time in modern history—
the first time that I can think of—there is a group of major powers to
which we belong whose relations are not marked by any great and

serious conflicts, by no conflicts, at least, that cannot be alleviated by patience, understanding, negotiation, and compromise. We have every reason to appreciate this situation, to cherish it, and to do all in our power to perpetuate it, remembering that good relations with great powers, like those with small ones, require constant attention and nurturing not only in crises but at all times. Here too we must be careful not to take our relations with great powers for granted, not to allow ourselves to be too heavily distracted by involvements in other parts of the world.

There is one other thing that I would like to mention about the various involvements that we have been concentrating on in the last two or three years. That is a very difficult one for me to talk about, for it's one on which one can be easily misunderstood: We have had a tendency to focus most of our efforts (or, it seems to me, a great many of them) on attempting to ensure democracy and human rights in other parts of the world. Though this ideal does credit to our own life and to our own aspirations and is one with which no one can argue, I must say that I don't think that all of the world is going to become democratic in our time no matter what we do. And I'm always a little afraid, a little disturbed, when I hear Americans talking to others about democracy and human rights because I always hear an undertone of self-congratulation, which I don't like. I don't like speaking down to people. In many instances the problems of other countries have been as severe as ours. And while we can tell them or can show them by example the way that we feel about these things, I think we should be very careful about telling them how to behave. One of the things that bothers me is that we have had a tendency to cast so many of these involvements in terms of our own struggle for democracy and human rights and done this in instances in which what we really should have been talking about (but which, for some curious reason, Americans never like to talk about) is simply our own national interest.

Not least among the problems that we have to handle in our relations with the major powers and some of the others as well is the continuing widespread development, cultivation, and prolif-eration of nuclear weapons and other weapons of mass destruc-tion. That is not merely a regional problem; it is a global one that involves a little less than the whole future of humanity and its stake in the future of civilization. I have never forgotten Robert Oppenheimer's reply when Ed Murrow asked him in a television interview whether humanity could survive a major nuclear war. "I don't know, I don't know," Oppenheimer replied. "But it would take the greatest act of faith to believe that what might survive it would be human." That remark, if anything, remains as true today as it was when Oppenheimer made it, for the control of this form of weaponry now rests in a larger number of hands. I believe that we, as the first country to have developed those weapons and the only one to use them against another population, and a largely helpless one at that, have a great and special responsibility and even a duty to take the lead in bringing those weapons under eventual control either through international organs or in having them eliminated from national arsenals.

Meeting this responsibility will require us to persuade others and to impose no small measure of restraint and scrutiny on our own words and actions. I welcome and commend the measures that we, the Russians, and others have undertaken recently. They are encouraging developments but are far from sufficient to meet the need. I greatly hope that we will now take a new look at this entire problem and will give to it the attention that it warrants. This is the least we can do for our children and our grandchildren.

There you have it: a voice from the century that is now passing to the inhabitants of the one about to begin. As always, when an older person tries to talk to younger people (and, believe me, practically everyone in this hall is younger than I), much of what he or she says is boring, for older people have a tendency to repeat themselves and talk about things seemingly removed from the interests and thoughts of their listeners. But it has been known to happen, here and there, that a small portion of what an oldster has had to say had relevance for the future as well as for the past. In this instance I leave that for you to judge. I cannot. I thank you for your attention.

---

AMERICAN LEADERSHIP, ISOLATIONISM,
AND UNILATERALISM[1]
JAMES R. SCHLESINGER[2]

---

The Center for Naval Analyses in Alexandria, Virginia, annually presents the Paul H. Nitze Award in recognition of important

[1]Delivered to the Center for Naval Analyses in Alexandria, Virginia on April 6, 1995.
[2]For biographical note see Appendix.

contributions to national and international security affairs. The 1995 recipient of the award was Dr. James R. Schlesinger.

Dr. Schlesinger, an experienced public servant, had served as Director of Intelligence and then Secretary of Defense in the Nixon and Ford administrations and later Secretary of Energy under President Carter. He was also a senior advisor at Lehman Brothers and for many years was associated with the Center for Strategic and International Studies at Georgetown University.

Dr. Schlesinger spoke on the topic "American Leadership, Isolationism, and Unilateralism." Senator Daniel Patrick Moynihan, in asking permission to inset Schlesinger's speech in the *Congressional Record,* described it as "an outstanding lecture," saying:

. . . when a scholar and public eminence of James Schlesinger's wisdom and stature addresses himself to an issue of such significance to world affairs, I believe it is incumbent on all of us to take notice. (*Congressional Record,* April 25, 1995, S5678)

*Dr. Schlesinger's speech:* Ladies and gentlemen: It is a special pleasure as well as an honor to have been chosen to receive the Paul H. Nitze Award. It is a special pleasure because Paul and I have been collaborating directly for almost a quarter of a century—and indirectly for even longer. I started working for Paul in the early 60's, when I was at the RAND Corporation, and he was head of International Security Affairs at the Pentagon. Years later when I was Secretary of Defense, Paul also worked for me. That clearly was the way it read on the organization chart, though, for those of you who may not be aware of this, such charts do not necessarily convey the whole of reality.

Of course, it is also a great honor for reasons that must be obvious—Paul's many contributions to this nation, his keenness of intellect (not the most common characteristic among high officials), his abiding role as a senior statesman. But perhaps one of Paul's most remarkable strengths is the cool and detached view that habitually he has taken with regard to national security affairs—rising above the hubbub of controversy. That characteristic has been displayed most prominently in matters such as the Palestine crisis of 1947, the Watergate crisis, and a "walk in the woods." Paul has displayed not only staying power, but (to avert to an issue that first brought us together) great throwweight in national security affairs. So it is a distinct honor as well as a personal pleasure to have been selected for this year's Nitze Award.

As most of us will recall, Paul Nitze was one of the principal authors of NSC—68, which, in the aftermath of World War II, charted that transformed role for the United States in international affairs—of leadership and continuous engagement. In a sense, the intellectual underpinnings of NSC—68 guided American policy for more than 40 years. But we all realize the era of NSC—68 is now over. It ended, rather abruptly, with the demise of the Soviet Union. Of course, it was Soviet misbehavior in the postwar world that formed the national consensus which gave sustenance to the design that underlay NSC—68. It manifested itself in the Greek-Turkish aid program, the Marshall Plan, the NATO Alliance—and, shortly later, the response to aggression in the Korean peninsula and the U.S.-Japan Security Treaty.

Yet, with the fall of the Soviet Union, this nation has been stripped both of guideposts to our foreign policy and of the national consensus that underpins that policy. Both the uncertainties and the challenges are substantial. This nation is deeply enmeshed in world affairs. For better or worse, it is the leading world power. No longer is it free, as it felt itself to be through much of its history, to stand aloof, to isolate itself from political events abroad. Yet, the clear guidelines that marked those past period of engagement are now lacking.

For this reason I want to spend some time this evening reflecting on American leadership, on isolationism, and on unilateralism. In his inaugural Nitze Award lecture, Sir Michael Howard looked back in time to review lessons from the Cold War period. I seek to look forward—to what comes next. Of late, one may have noticed the demands for "American leadership" and the charges of "isolationist" that have reverberated across the political landscape. That the charge of "isolationist" is so widely used as a political epithet reveals that the notion that America can stand aloof has little resonance with the American public. The public fully accepts that its economic ties, its political interests, even its residual vulnerability in an era of nuclear weapons, preclude a wholesale American withdrawal from international affairs. Moreover, even if we could stand aside, the voice of conscience insists that it would not be right for America to be indifferent to political travail, particularly when it affects long-time allies of the United States.

By contrast to these rejected charges of isolationism, the image of American leadership has a grand resonance. Unhappy events overseas, whether or not there is any serious American interest, are regularly blamed on the "failure of American leadership." Everybody seems to urge American leadership. Americans like to flatter themselves with the notion that this country is the "sole surviving superpower"—and expect action to make those unhappy events go away—so long as it does not cost us very much. Our European allies—sometimes rightly, sometimes wrongly—have demanded: Where is American leadership? (Of late that cry has diminished in intensity, as European expectations regarding American leadership have faded.) Our Asian associates have resented our continuous preaching, yet all are concerned that an erosion over time of American power in the Pacific will allow an instability from which until now they have been protected. Preachers, teachers, editorial writers, if not little children in the street, seem to presuppose American leadership—but fundamentally treat it as a panacea—as a ready antidote for most, if not all, of the world's problems.

Thus, the real issue comes down, not to withdrawal or isolation—those are epithets—but to when, where, and how we choose to intervene. In part the charge of isolation really comes down to a suspicion of unilateral moves by the United States on the international scene. For those who embrace multilateralism and who prefer to work through international bodies, the charge of isolationist comes readily as a riposte to those who do not agree with them. But multilateralism can readily be a cover for inaction. It can also be, and frequently is, a vehicle for ineffective action. Of course, those who instinctively prefer to work through international bodies are frequently right that their opponents are short sighted or even blindly chauvinistic. But their actions are scarcely isolationist. Rightly or wrongly, they are regularly intended to achieve international objectives. But such unilateralist impulses may be equally flawed or ineffective.

The Clinton administration has chided its foes for being isolationists. It is perhaps merely the most recent assertion of "assertive multilateralism." Their critics, in turn, have responded in kind. The administration may fervently believe in the collaboration among nations, yet it has shown a distinct proclivity to become embroiled in quarrels with individual nations, sometimes including old allies, over issues which are either only remotely our business or over which our influence is modest. Endangering ties with those that have been reliable allies, along with ineffectual, if irritating, advocacy of policies over which our influence is slight runs the risk of weakening the ties between ourselves and other nations—in effect isolating the United States. In terms of its accolades to international engagement, the administration is clearly beyond criticism. It is only those specific actions that the administration takes, which properly comes out and which understandably alarms its critics. Irrespective of the good intentions, such actions may weaken the international position of the United States.

Thus, the question is not one of isolation or withdrawal. The question is where, when, and on what terms does the United States become engaged. What is our foreign policy to be—now that the conceptually easy task of containment has come to an end. It is perhaps unnecessary to remind this audience that such questions are antecedent to the issue of shaping our military forces. The shaping of those forces depends upon the role that the United States wishes to play in the world—and the circumstances under which those forces may become engaged.

Thus, we seek a new paradigm for an effective foreign policy. We seek, in effect, a successor to NSC—68. But it is not easy to come by. Some of the difficulty in finding that new paradigm is inherent. It is probably unavoidable that we flounder to some degree at historic turning points. We did so after World War II. It was not until 1947–1948 that we began to find our bearings—and to do that we had the indispensable help of Joseph Stalin. Now the international scene is vastly more complex and yet there is much less direct danger to the United States. Though there are numerous eruptions on the international scene, there is little to concentrate the mind.

In every such eruption, somewhere someone will call on the United States to do something. "Concentrating the mind" is indispensable to some degree. It is better that we recognize that simple fact rather than having reality thrust upon us. No nation can do everything; we would be wise not to aspire to do so.

I can recall over 40 years ago listening to a debate at Harvard regarding the resolution of one of our seemingly perennial steel strikes—during which John Dunlop, later Secretary of Labor, commented: "It is important for a democracy not too frequently to demonstrate its own ineffectiveness." I have never forgotten that injunction. But what is true for domestic policy is even more true for foreign policy. Becoming engaged in numerous disputes, particularly if one lacks public backing, is the high road to ineffectiveness.

Perhaps it is obvious to say that the problem is especially difficult for the United States, which, as a world power, might find its attention drawn in any one of many directions—and for which public backing is a sometime thing and must be carefully fostered.

In the past and for other great powers, the choice of foreign policy tendered to be far simpler. For most it was geographically determined. There likely would be an historic enemy. For, say, France or Germany, there was little uncertainty as to who one's foe might be and where one must be prepared to fight. To be sure, for Britain, whose imperial interests were more far-flung, the problem was broader: to protect communications with the empire and to prevent any single power from dominating the continent. Yet for the United States today, our interests are even more diverse, and the challenge of being a world power has grown since the era of European dominance.

Moreover, the task was far easier in another respect. Given what was seen as clear national interests, the unquestioned rule for the European powers stressed the priority to be assigned to foreign policy. The phrase from Bismarckian German puts it simply: das Primat der Aussenpolitik—the primacy of foreign policy. Yet, the primacy was far easier to establish in a dynastic regime. Even in the case of England, the problem was not insuperable— in light of its clearly defined foreign policy, the preservation of the balance of power, and a continued willingness of the British public to defer to a strong governing class.

But here in the United States we now show signs of turning das Primat der Aussenpolitik on its head and allowing foreign policy to be determined by domestic politics. In any democracy that is a continuing temptation; it is particularly a problem in the United States where the vicissitudes of public opinion can so easily determine public policy. And, particularly is this so in the absence of an overriding fear (as with the Soviet Union) or an overriding anger as with Japan or Spain in an earlier era (remember Pearl Harbor, remember the Maine). In sustaining public support, "it is frequently helpful if the anger has focused on a weak foe (Mexico, Spain, or Grenada) for then one can count on public exultation in a "glorious little war."

When, however, there is no clear and formidable foe and when only a few Middle Eastern countries seem to generate public anger, it is difficult to sustain a priority in foreign policy (as George Bush belatedly discovered). It is thus seductively easy to accept the primary of domestic politics.

In addition to the absence of a clear focus and the existence of diverse areas of potential responsibility for the United States, which alone is a world power, there is a further problem. There are too many distractions, most of them transitory in nature. It is difficult to concentrate on those issues that might represent "permanent interests," given the worldwide domain of television with a power, if not an agenda, that exceeds that of "yellow journalism" in the past. Rather than permanent interests, we experience sudden passionate interest in the Bosnians, the Kurds, the Rwandans, the flight of Haitian or Cuban refugees, then the Kurds again that lasts a few weeks or months at most—until the story pales, the public tires of it, and then moves on. Surely that complicates the task of selecting those interests and issues to which we should adhere. It makes the challenge of sustaining support for long term interests, as opposed to momentary distractions, immensely difficult.

Need I add that these factors also make immensely difficult the task of force planning. There is uncertainty as to what our foreign policy may be. Consequently, there is an uncertainty as to where we might fight. Choosing two major regional conflicts as "representative" is hardly an ideal solution—reminding us of the locale of past conflicts rather than of the likely future conflicts. Moreover, under these circumstances there are genuine conflicts regarding specific foreign objectives. With respect to our Asian policies, for example, the DOD's International Security Affairs opines: "the United States remains dedicated to strengthening alliances and friendships." Yet, this scarcely describes the motives that guide the actions of the U.S. Trade Representative, who is predisposed to confrontations with the same Asian states—by implicitly, if not explicitly, threatening to weaken those alliances and friendships. In U.S. policy there is a growing mixture of economic rivalry and alliance reassurance. Perhaps this is unavoidable, yet clearly it undercuts any joint planning with those allies on whom we should be able to count.

I have now devoted some time to explaining why in this postwar world the inherent difficulties for this nation shaping its foreign policy have grown. Now let me turn to analyzing how our own actions have been compounding those difficulties inherent in this altered world—and have seemed to undercut that role of world leader which we ostensibly cherish. But first I must portray the general behavior and the style necessary to sustain the role of world leader. One does not require any special knowledge or erudition to understand these requirements; they should be obvious to any long time observer of politics.

First, to be accepted as a leader, a nation must be seen not to be acting primarily for its own account. It must understand and take into account the interests of its followers. It must also be seen to be genuinely interested in international affairs—rather than blindly follow the dictates of its own domestic politics and it must focus on matters of real consequence.

Second, it must be reasonably consistent. Changes in policy should be few in number—and taken for what are seen as valid reasons. One must be steadfast. A great power does not lightly enter into commitments, but when it does so it must be with the serious intent of carrying them out. In brief those who wish to retain a position of leadership must avoid capriciousness. Otherwise one's credibility rapidly diminishes, and one's influence fades with almost equal rapidity.

Of late the United States has failed to observe these obvious rules. While we flatter ourselves as the world's sole remaining superpower, we seem to be amazed that our influence seems to be shrinking. To be sure, some such shrinkage is inherent in the change of circumstances. With the demise of the Soviet threat, other nations, previously dependent upon the United States for protection, are now less dependent and so less inclined to defer to our wishes. But the erosion of our influence proceeds more rapidly than required by the circumstances. If we are to arrest that decline, we must understand the causes.

If a nation is to lead, it must seem to be genuinely concerned about international affairs—and not driven primarily by domestic pressures. Nonetheless, in recent years our policies being driven by domestic constituencies appear to be the rule rather than the exception. In Northern Ireland, in Haiti, in respect to Cuba or Haitian refugees, in much of the Middle East, our policies seem to be driven by domestic pressures—and we appear largely indifferent regarding the international repercussions. A hungerstrike and pressures from the Black Caucus brought a shift in our policies toward Haiti. A senior official backgrounds to the press that: "No one will get to the right of us on Iran." The President's National Security Advisor reveals that the United States will attempt once again to tighten sanctions on Libya by persuading our European partners to cease buying Libyan oil. This revelation occurs, not in a regular diplomatic forum, but in a meeting with the families of the victims of Pan Am 108.

Disappointed as they may have been, Europeans were not really surprised that the United States did not regard Bosnia as primarily our business. (Especially was this so in light of the European Union's having previously told us that Europe would handle Bosnia, and there was no need for our intervention.) They were, however, non-plussed that we would regard the affairs of Northern Ireland as primarily our business. Northern Ireland is, after all, a province of the United Kingdom, part of its sovereign territory. For us to butt in (no other expression seems suitable!) for domestic political reasons appeared both ignorant and bumptious. Such behavior is scarcely consistent with the solidarity of NATO, let alone the "special relationship." I cannot overstate the dismay of other Europeans regarding our treatment of the British. The general reaction is: If the Americans will behave this way to their most intimate partner, what can the rest of us expect? The diplomat's word for this episode is: "disappointment."

This administration is explicitly vulnerable to the conservative charge that it is soft—most notably soft on Saddam Hussein. For this reason it seeks, with ever lessening support and growing desperation to maintain the sanctions on Iraq that were adopted in 1990. Three of the five permanent members of the Security Council have now introduced a resolution to terminate those sanctions. Even Iraq's neighbors regard our policy as no longer productive, though they are reluctant to say so to our highest officials. If the United States is seen primarily for domestic political reasons to be stretching our sanctions believed to be unproductive, if not unjust, how ready will others again be to follow American leadership in imposing sanctions? The answer is clear. A willingness to put domestic pressures in front of international considerations will undermine the very multilateral mechanisms that the administration believes ideal for abiding international stability. Indeed, with respect to Libya, Iran, and Iraq, rather than achieving its declared goal isolating those countries, our diplomacy tends to isolate the United States itself.

The effect of these altogether too many cases of putting domestic politics first is to obscure those instances in which the administration has rightly focused our policies on the longer term interests both of this nation and of international stability—most notably our relations with Russia and the spread of nuclear weapons. Other nations doubt that we understand their interests, let alone take them into adequate account. When the United States proclaims that providing (6000 thermal megawatts of) light water reactors to North Korea is the best remedy for curbing North Korea's drive to acquire nuclear weapons, it makes it somewhat difficult, to say the least, to persuade the Russians that providing light water reactors in Iran creates an open road to nuclear spread. To be effective, even with respect to common long-term interests, a leader needs to maintain its credibility.

The problem goes well beyond the administration. One can think of many advantages of divided government—invetting domestic proposals. However, I myself can think of virtually no advantages in divided government with respect to international affairs. It weakens the voice of any administration—and it undermines the credibility of American diplomacy. This Congress now seems inclined to inflict on the Clinton administration's policies regarding Bosnia and regarding Russian aid the same kind of cavalier treatment with which its Democratic predecessor treated President Bush's policies toward China after Tiananmen Square. Whatever the merits or defects of our policy on the so-called Mexican bail out or toward Iran, Congressional intervention does not seem likely to improve them.

Our policies have been changeable rather than consistent. Our commitments do not appear to be reliable. Our policies appear excessively driven by domestic constituencies. The result is that the call for American leadership is diminishing in strength. Increasingly American leadership appears to be a problem rather than a solution.

We are tempting fate. Some years ago Paul Nitze suggested that "other nations can be expected to coalesce to cut us down to size." Unless we are prepared to deflect our own domestic pressures, to take international considerations primarily into account, to understand the differing interests of other nations, and to pursue worthy long-term, common interests, we shall regrettably accelerate that process. Writing in 1950 in his splendid work, "American Diplomacy," George Kennan observed: "history does not forgive us our national mistakes because they are explicable in terms of our domestic politics." He also states: "A nation which excuses its own failures by the same sacred untouchableness of its own habits can excuse itself into complete disaster."

With the end of the totalitarian threat, with the remarkably changed international circumstances, the danger to the United States has visibly receded, and there is little likelihood of a "complete disaster." Nonetheless, despite the lessened danger, the possibility remains of cumulative small setbacks and the erosion of our position. We may ignore such possibilities—and it is unlikely to be fatal. Still the rules are quite simple. To be a leader, a nation must sustain its credibility.

Ladies and Gentlemen, you have been more than patient. I must draw to a close—and must also offer a few conclusions.

During the Cold War the stakes were immense: the preservation of the Western democracies and, if I may say so, the substantial preservation of Western Civilization itself of which the United States was the security mainstay. (I say this despite the probable assault of the multiculturalists.) But with the end of the cohesion and menace of the Soviet empire, the stakes have now shrunken. The United States, the world's most powerful nation, is in a sense free to be capricious, to be irresponsible. Yet, it will not soon fall into direct and serious danger. Nonetheless, there are restraints—and there are prospective consequences of our actions. The price of capriciousness will inevitably be a loss of credibility—and of our position of leadership.

While the United States is a powerful country, it is not all-powerful. At the close of the nineteenth century, Secretary of State Richard Olney could declaim during the Venezuelan dispute with Great Britain that the United States' "word was flat on this continent." Whatever we may wish, it is *not* flat around the world. To pretend otherwise will make us look foolish. The focus of our foreign policy concern, as Paul Nitze has said, should be "what kind of relations among the leading powers." We must be cautious about involving ourselves in matters of lesser consequences. We should be restrained in word as well as deed. The United States is not obliged to comment on everything. Meddling in issues in which our interests are only tangentially involved, nagging others about their defects, real or imaginary, may make us feel good for the moment. It is not the road to successful or long-term leadership.

To provide long-term leadership, other nations must understand that we do not speak casually or loosely. When we do choose to make a commitment, other nations need to know that we can and probably will live up to it. Always remember: leadership is not an inheritance; it must be earned anew, each decade, each year.

# REAFFIRMING VALUES

## THE ARTS AND EDUCATION[1]
### JANE ALEXANDER[2]

"God help the government that meddles with art," proclaimed Lord Melbourne, British Prime Minister more than 150 years ago. Many Americans were beginning to agree with that sentiment following the prolonged controversy surrounding federal funding for the arts. The controversy began in 1989 when conservative members of Congress discovered that federal funds provided by the National Endowment for the Arts had been given to two artists, Robert Mapplethorpe and Andres Serrano. Mapplethorpe's photographic exhibitions depicted explicit homosexual themes; one piece of art by Serrano consisted of a crucifix submerged in urine. Debate raged between those who argued that any censorship of the NEA was wrong no matter how disagreeable some might find the works it supported and others who wanted to prevent the NEA from supporting similar controversial art projects. The battle continued for more than five years and led to the resignation of NEA director John Frohnmayer. (For comments related to the controversy, see speeches by John Frohnmayer in *Representative American Speeches 1990–1991* and *1991–1992.*

Following the resignation of Frohnmayer, Jane Alexander was appointed the head of the NEA. In this role, Alexander, a distinguished television, film, and theater actress and recipient of many acting, humanitarian, and cultural awards, sought to reduce the passions surrounding the agency.

On May 20, 1994, Alexander delivered the main address at the 89th commencement exercises of the Julliard School in New York, a school devoted to training students in the arts. Drawing on her own experiences, both as a student and a performer, Alexander argued that regardless of their futures the graduates would benefit from their study of the arts. Alexander spoke to 214

[1]Delivered at the commencement exercises of the Julliard School in Alice Tully Hall in New York City on May 20, 1994 at 11:00 a.m.
[2]For biographical note see Appendix.

graduates and their guests, faculty, and the media, an audience of about nine hundred people in Alice Tully Hall at 11:00 A.M. During the ceremonies, the Julliard School awarded honorary doctorate degrees to Alexander and Garth Fagan, Marilyn Horne, June Noble Larkin, and Andee Watts.

*Ms. Alexander's speech:* Thank you for that kind introduction. Shakespeare has a great expression for this time in your life. He has Cleopatra in *Antony and Cleopatra* call these "My salad days, when I was green in judgment." Looking out at those of you graduating today, I see a lot of green faces, and as a friend named Kermit said, "It's not easy being green." But it is fitting, perhaps, that we hold these commencements in the springtime when life is beginning and the world is green with promise. The very word commencement means beginning.

When I was in my salad days, I was accepted at the Columbia University School of Drama during my senior year in high school. In March of that spring semester, the school closed suddenly, and I was forced to make other plans. I have always regretted that I didn't have the opportunity for the kind of intensive training in the arts that you have enjoyed. What has been the value of your daily immersion in the arts? What kind of artists, indeed what kind of citizens will you become?

This occasion lends itself to speculation, to the bittersweet. The poet Samuel Hazo writes about life's journey in a poem called "The First and Only Sailing," of which I'll quote the last few lines:

> Expect nothing,
> and anything seems everything.
> Expect everything, and anything
> seems nothing . . .
> To live
> you leave your yesterselves
> to drown without a funeral.
> You chart a trek where no
> one's sailed before.
> You rig.
> You anchor up.
> You sail.

Your time at Juilliard has been spent learning when to tack or when to open your sails to the wind; it has been filled with hard work and wild ideas, friendship, love, the camaraderie of community. As you sail into tomorrow, you won't find another place or another time quite like it. I learned more about ancient Egypt and

Rome from *Antony and Cleopatra* than any course in history; it gave me perspectives on history, literature, and music. I learned about the emotional reality of life that only art addresses. This place has given you the chance to know yourselves from the inside out. And that knowledge is more valuable than the actual recitals, the acting lessons, or discovering the difference between andante and adagio, between a plié and a pirouette.

So you anchor up and you set sail. What will become of you? Two Sundays ago, on *60 Minutes,* the programs here at Juilliard were profiled. There are many courses to follow for a life in the arts. Some of you in this room will realize your dream and earn your living in your discipline. Those of you who wish to go on to become performing artists face a daunting task. Society throws up roadblocks all the time—intolerance, misunderstanding, indifference, neglect. Let's face it, the financial rewards have never been great, except for a small percentage of artists who are very successful. And the artist and society have a tentative relationship, often wary of one another, for the artist is sometimes the sentinel on the precipice, heralding change as it peeks over the horizon. Artists challenge, ask difficult questions, and rattle our cages. They can make our skin itch, our souls bristle, and they can touch us to our heart's deep core.

Even without roadblocks, it still takes hard work, talent and perseverance to make art. It takes tools, time and opportunity to achieve excellence, even when the tool is as simple as a pencil or paper, and the time as rare as the morning hours before you trudge off to work. That is why we at the Endowment are committed to supporting the individual artist through our fellowships. We buy time for the promise of excellence.

One of the most painful things I have had to do as chairman was announce the suspension of our Professional Training grants in the NEA's Theater Program. The Juilliard drama school suffered a loss of $25,000 with this cutback, but over the past 15 years, the Arts Endowment has lost 46 percent of its purchasing power, and the demand for our grants increases daily. Faced with rising administrative costs and a $4.7 million cut to our budget this year, we reduced all our programs. Our Theater Program had to cut $250,000 from its budget, and we suspended funding in the Professional Theater Training category, so that we could preserve as much money as possible for the theater companies across this country, many of which are struggling to stay afloat. In the years ahead we hope to have more money and will reinstate this program which is so beneficial to students here at Juilliard and in other schools for the arts. But it does little good to receive theater training if there aren't theaters in which to work. We have stretched the federal dollar to the snapping point, and in many arts disciplines, the flat budget of the Endowment and other funding sources has made the difficult task of earning a living as an artist even more daunting.

Those of you with iron wills and talent will persevere, as you should. This immersion at Juilliard has let you know where you stand in relationship to other talented people and will help you set the course for your sailing. Or in the words of Bernard Malamud, "If you are a genius, assert yourself, in arts and humanity." By all mean, but even those not labelled genius can succeed through perseverance in the face of rejection and through daily work at your art.

Others of you will become an influence in the lives of many students through teaching. My niece, who studies music at Trinity College in Dublin, knew fairly early on that she didn't want to be a performing artist, she wanted to teach. She made a conscious choice out of a desire to open the doors to art, creativity and imagination to others. She has 13 young students already and has paid her way through college. A truly good and wise teacher is a lasting gift, as rare as a true artist. Teachers do more than lecture and give grades; in the best sense, they are mentors, taking us by the hand to unlock the mysteries behind our own creativity. A great teacher is a friend to your intellect, to your potential, to your imagination and will be with you in your mind's eye for life. A salute to the teachers, here at Juilliard now and to the future teachers in this graduating class!

Still others of you may go on to careers that are not directly related to your years here. My own gene pool indicated that I was destined for a career in medicine. My grandfather, Daniel Quigley, was a doctor, in Nebraska, personal physician of Buffalo Bill. My mother was a nurse, and my father a doctor and professor at Harvard Medical School. I am sure that if you asked any of them gathered around my cradle, none would have predicted a career in the theater for me. Nor could I have predicted that I would leave the theatre for politics. So who knows what is in store for you? You may be administrators or you may decide to seek your living in some other profession—from homemaker to going on to medical school. It's not as unlikely as it seems. Anton Chekhov was a doctor and a playwright, as is Jonathan Miller. William Carlos

Williams was a doctor and a poet. Wallace Stevens, one of the great American poets of this century, worked for the Hartford Insurance Company all of his life, and my favorite, Emily Dickinson, rarely left her home in Amherst.

No matter what you do, you will feel the ripple effect of this education in the arts, this total engagement with creativity. All of us begin as imaginative beings, and it is fate or circumstance that leads us to hold onto or let go of creativity and imagination. Children naturally curious explore their worlds, listening, touching, communicating as they learn, and if that environment includes the arts, they will be in tune with the aesthetic side of life from the very beginning. Those of you who become parents will take the lessons you learned from Juilliard—the value of the arts—and give your children a priceless gift.

You will carry the arts with you wherever you go. They will affect how you think and act and respond to others—children, family, friends and acquaintances. I contend that the arts will make you better people, more compassionate citizens, more tolerant and understanding. For the arts demonstrate most clearly our connectedness, our common human nature. They speak to what unites us all under the skin, to the human spirit in all our pain and joy, our disenchantment and beguilement, our anger and our celebration.

As students who have spent the past few years together absorbed in the arts, you are indelibly stamped with creativity. Many people think artists are a little different, a bit touched. Even Shakespeare coupled the poet with the lunatic and the lover in a sort of unstable trinity of neurotics. Of course, other inquiries have debunked the notion that creative people are motivated by neurosis. Artists and creative thinkers are, in Anthony Storr's book *The Dynamics of Creation,* motivated by a *"divine discontent . . . man's discontent is his most precious attribute."* Artists imagine different worlds, better worlds.

It is perhaps fitting here that we acknowledge the passing of Jacqueline Kennedy Onassis whose grace and beauty encouraged the same in all aspects of society. As First Lady, Jackie Kennedy invited the great artists of the age to the White House for performances. She established a White House Fine Arts Committee, hired the first White House curator, and helped preserve such historic buildings as the Old Executive Office Building next to the White House. Her dream was to establish a federal Department of the Arts, which became realized in a slightly different version as the Arts Endowment. The writer Carl Anthony said, "She felt American culture was as good as European culture . . . most people have never fully appreciated how richly she contributed to the quality of American life in terms of bringing the arts and humanities to the American landscape." Her legacy is that she brought grace and imagination to her role, and she was instrumental in getting this country to realize the importance of culture and the arts to our daily lives. She believed in a better world.

Because we believe in better worlds at the National Endowment for the Arts, we are today working with artists and art organizations all across the country to reach out to people in our communities to get them to re-connect to the power of the arts to transcend our differences. We are working with other federal agencies to make sure that the arts are included on the agenda as the administration seeks holistic solutions to the problems our society faces. We are working with school districts to make sure the arts are included in the curriculum so that our children may be equipped with the imagination, creativity and open minds necessary not only to succeed in the world of tomorrow, but to live more harmoniously with one another. We are working for you and for your fellow citizens to advance the arts in this country to shore up our art institutions and to make possible the conditions where you—as artists and teachers and imaginative thinkers— may compose your life and pursue your vision.

Whatever you do, do what you love. Carry the arts with you wherever the voyage may take you, and you will leave Juilliard with the maps to guide you on that journey. If you have the call to be an artist, that vision is vital to your dream. And if you have the call to some other kind of life, that vision will be sharper and clearer through the arts.

I'd like to close with one of my favorite quotes of the great Norwegian playwright Henrik Ibsen, because I think those of us in the performing arts, be it theater, dance, music, or opera, share a special and unique charter in the world of art: we dedicate our lives to the execution of the very best we have to give at the moment of live performance—a lesson perhaps how we all might live our lives on a daily basis moment to moment.

Some say that the art of the theatre, born for and bound to the moment, must, like a soap bubble or nocturnal meteor, dazzle, then burst and leave no trace. Free yourself from this dark thought! The very fact that your art is a child of fragrance, of the spirit, of a mood, of personality and imagination, and not something of wood and stone, or even a thought fixed in black and white, but a sprite forever swinging free on beauty's vine, the fact that it lacks tangible form, renders it immune to the gnawing of time's worm. And that is what life truly means: to live in memory . . . to rest in people's minds free of the mildew and rust of age . . . and this lot has been granted to you.

Bon voyage! And thank you.

---

## WILLIAM FAULKNER'S OLD VERITIES: IT'S PLANTING TIME IN AMERICA[1]
### JACK J. VALENTI[2]

---

Outstanding speeches that do not command national media coverage often are inserted in the *Congressional Record* by members of Congress who believe the speaker's remarks deserve the attention of other Congressmen and the general public. One such address was the first Louis Nizer lecture delivered by the Jack Valenti, president and CEO of the Motion Picture Association of America and a former aide to President Lyndon B. Johnson.

Senator William S. Cohen of Maine inserted Valenti's lecture in the *Congressional Record,* noting that Valenti's words that evening carried special meaning for him and, he thought, for others as well:

They are words of optimism about our future in a time when many in our country do not feel optimistic. But they are also words of caution, directed toward all of us in this body, and all of us in this city, who create the policies under which Americans live. They stress the importance of the family of education, of appropriate moral conduct, of individual—not governmental—responsibility. They are words to which we should all give careful consideration. (*Congressional Record,* January 24, 1995, S1384)

Valenti chose to discuss as the subject of his lecture the "old verities" found in William Faulkner's acceptance speech for the Nobel Prize for Literature in 1950.

*Mr. Valenti's speech:* The issues of liberty and the replenishment of community values stirred restlessly within Louis Nizer. He and I talked often about the compass course of the society. We both had

[1]The first Louis Nizer Lecture delivered in New York City on January 24, 1995.
[2]For biographical note see Appendix.

read the purifying speech of William Faulkner when he received
the Nobel Prize for Literature, on December 10, 1950. Like me,
Louis found in Faulkner's words a dark punishing wisdom, a
plain, spare design for civic conduct. It is from Faulkner's vision
that what I say tonight has taken wings. I think Louis would
approve. Let me begin, then, by admiring this man, Louis Nizer,
who has drawn so many of you here tonight.

In the muscular and musical English language which Louis
knew so well, loved so much and illuminated so elegantly, there
exist two words which perfectly describe him.

They are "polymath" and "fidelity."

Polymath means an artisan of immense learning in many
fields.

Francis Bacon once said he had taken all knowledge to be his
province. For Bacon it was not an immodest objective. But such
were Louis Nizer's vast and diverse talents, he is the only man I
know or knew who could come close to matching Francis Bacon.
Lawyer, courtroom genius, public speaker, best selling author,
painter, composer, lyricist, historian, counselor to presidents and
public officials, he was all of these and more. And in each he
performed with excelling intellect and ascending success.

Fidelity means faithfulness to obligations and observances.

Louis Nizer gave special meaning to the word "fidelity." In his
binding to the law, fidelity took on a richer meaning. The law in
all its glory was the core of his life. It was the reservoir from which
his daily tasks drew nourishment.

I first met Louis Nizer almost twenty-nine years ago when he
came to visit with me in my office in the White House. I was about
to resign as Special Assistant to the President, to become the
President of the Motion Picture Association of America. He was
to become the MPAA general counsel. Our paths that day not
only crossed, but became intimately interwoven and forever
sealed in friendship and trust.

His long, fruitful life is now over. Death, as it does to every
mortal, has finally come to Louis Nizer. I can say that I am so
grateful to a beneficent God that I was given to know Louis so
intimately, so gloriously, so lovingly. He was a noble man. There
are so few of his kind.

Any enterprise that bears Louis' name is valuable to me. This
evening then, to me, has great worth. May the Louis Nizer Lecture series flourish in the decades ahead. May I do it as little
damage as possible tonight.

I have been fortunate to spend my entire working career in two of life's fascinations, politics and movies. I have worked the precincts of my native Texas, within City Hall and county courthouses and the state capitol. I have been privy to decision making in the White House, at the side of a brave, extraordinary President. And I have for a long time been among and within the creative and executive communities of Hollywood and the world cinema.

Both arenas, movies and politics, are sprung from the same DNA. Their aims are the same: to entice voters and audiences to yield to their persuasions. What is the value of those persuasions? What is real? What is right? What is truth? Who determines it? Who furnishes the boundaries for the daily moral grind of a functioning society? How is that society to be governed? How do you shape a foundation for a nation's prime objective to endure, always striving to reach for the ascending curve?

These are ancient queries. Answers are available but often they are porous, not readily translated into specific behavior. Sometimes they are cast in different shapes to different people. Which answer is true? "What is truth," said jesting Pilate, and would not stay for an answer.

I have thought a lot about this, though thinking about these matters is like trying to pick up mercury with a fork. It is maddeningly elusive. But we have to keep trying.

Herodotus tells the story of Athenians so emotionally affected by the drama, "The Capture of Miletus," by the poet Phrynichus, that the whole theater wept openly. When their passions had cooled, Athenian officials passed a law forbidding Phrynichus ever again to offer this play to the public. He was fined a thousand drachmas for reminding his fellows citizens of their own sorrows. It is an apt metaphor for our current scene. Nothing so much describes the perversity of political and social conduct, and calls to judgment the resorting to morality by public officials as an instrument of domestic and foreign policy.

It's a dicey political game to play. Like the Athenians we are deeply involved in that which tugs at both our practical minds and our moral conscience. Also like the Athenians we find the real world, the morning after, not so desirable as we had previously thought.

If morality is a rostrum from which we survey our lives, then it is also a principle on which we stand. Principles, unless one rises above them, are cruelly steadfast. If a principle is ignored, for whatever practical reasons, or bent, for whatever seemingly rational decision, then it is no longer a principle. It becomes a weak reed on which we lean at our own peril.

So it is that Presidents and Members of Congress, as well as officials of state and local governments, find themselves dealing with morality on a "yes, but" logic. If you tried to draw up a catalogue of the good guys and the bad guys, you wind up with public officials from the President down being judged on the same basis as that well known medieval monarch, Philip the Good, renowned in his time for both the number of his bastards and the piety of his fasts. Too often our officials, in both political parties, see issues through their own personal prism. To that end, the historian Procopius wrote about the Emperor Justinian: "He didn't think that the slaying of men was murder unless they happened to share his own religious view."

We are poised for a great debate in this land. It has to do with the reach of government, how wide, how narrow. But I daresay the debate will be waged on the wrong platform. Emerson may have gotten it right when he wrote: "God offers to everyone his choice between truth and repose. Take what you please, you can never have both." Emerson is also speaking to this generation as well.

I am not a pessimist. Never have been. Don't intend to start now. This country did not survive more than 200 years of cruel disjointings to be undone at this particular moment by discomforts cataloged at length, mainly by TV commentators and political consultants. These are the new political Druids who convince their viewers and their clients that they alone are capable of inspecting the entrails of a pig and thereby are solely in possession of the bewitchery which will lead voters to a proper decision.

But this scrambling, unquiet, violent time is one of the rare moments in our history when those who govern us and those who are governed are in concert. Fear is the scarlet thread which runs like a twanging wire through the nation. Fear of tomorrow; fear of losing one's job; fear that children will find their future less attractive than did their parents; fear of crime, in the neighborhoods and in the home; fear that the old bindings which held the nation together are snapping: in too many cities there are too many broken homes, too much loss of the affection which thickens family ties, too much crazy drug use and users, too many guns in the hands of too many children, too many babies having babies, abandonment of the church, schools without discipline, life without hope, anger fed by imagined slights and bigoted blights.

No wonder there is fear. The first thing we have to do to

combat fear is understand that no matter how well intentioned we are, unless we are guided by a basic moral compass, we will neither begin nor finish the journey. Make no mistake, the politicians are listening. There is nothing so compelling to a public official as the angry buzz of the local multitudes.

Therefore (ah, 'Therefore' is a wondrous word. It says enough of the rhetoric, what do you do tomorrow morning?), Therefore:

We ought to start with William Faulkner. In his speech in 1950, he cited what he called "the old universal verities and truth of the heart, the old universal truth lacking which any story is ephemeral and doomed—love and honor and pity and pride and compassion and sacrifice." He might have added "and duty and loyalty and service to one's family and friends and country."

Faulkner's old verities have weight because they are what an enduring nation is all about. Old fashioned words? Yes, they are. Long-living words? Yes, they are. All the more reason why words which have sustained themselves in myth and reality are never out of date. These words describe neither religion nor ideology nor political affiliation. No group or faction or political party has a monopoly on interpreting their meaning.

What Faulkner's verities represent is a code of conduct between human beings, between the citizen and the state, between neighbors, friends, associates. They are better guides than a political poll, or the blatherings demagogues, or those earnest folks who insist they alone possess God's wisdom. We have an old prayer in Texas when we encounter these human repositories of divine Truth: "Dear Lord, let me seek the truth, but spare me the company of those who have found it." Nice prayer. I say it often.

So, we begin with Faulkner's proposition that there are basics deep rooted in those crevices where each of us stores our beliefs and our passions. Without them we are barren of aim or cause or reason. Or as Faulkner said, without them we "labor under a curse."

Government cannot, ought not, be a national nanny, nor the custodian of our faith nor the divine arbiter of our lives. Each citizen must be responsible for his or her actions, fathers, mothers, sons, daughters. Parents must be responsible for their children. Adults responsible for their decisions. Young people responsible for what they do. Playing "victim," copping a plea that "the Devil made me do it," these are mocking charades in which the foolish listen to the dunces and the dimwits lead the mob.

Taking responsibility for one's life, for one's action, does not mean turning away from the helpless and the hopeless. What it does mean is that if there is not a civic commitment to be individually responsible, the future is pockmarked with detours and disappointment. But we must be wary in the months ahead. Strenuous efforts will be made to amputate the national government's intervention in the lives of those pressed against the wall because of circumstances over which they have no control. It would be tragic to do that. It would be worse than a crime. It would be a blunder. It cannot be allowed to happen.

To give Faulkner's old verities a communal reality, we have to begin within the family, for parents to care enough, believe enough, do enough to begin the process. Parents, sufficiently armed with passion, can do the most.

Alongside this familial commitment has to be a zealous attention to teachers and schools. We have to be willing to pay for first class public education or it continues to be lousy education. We can't build enough prisons, or wield enough judicial sabers, or legislate enough tough death penalty laws to compensate for the collapse of discipline in the classroom, or the graduation from high school of too many who can't read or write or the total loss of Faulkner's verities. In a time when our national obligations are larger than our capacity to fulfill them all at the same time, our leaders must make it clear—painful, discomforting, frustrating as it may be—that we have to reinstall the family and the school and the church as the central teaching centers for young people. We have to begin the journey back into ourselves before we can go forward into our future. Too idealistic? Too namby-pamby? Too impossible? 'Yes,' to all of those descriptions if you think a society can just amble along and keep its liberties alive when so much of its core convictions are in a state of decay. I don't. Every day liberty must be guarded, because like virtue it is every day besieged.

Then, why am I optimistic? Because all things are always in flux. Nothing lasts forever, neither triumph nor tragedy, nor the omissions of the human spirit. So long as we understand who we are, why we are what we are, and how we became so, then we will always be able to know where it is that we ought to turn and where we must go. Of course, this requires a national conviction. Without conviction, said Lord Macaulay, a man or woman will be right only by accident.

President Kennedy supposedly told the story of a French general in Algeria who wanted to plant a special kind of tree to line the road to his chateau. "But," protested his gardener, "that tree takes a 100 years to bloom." The general smiled and said: "Then we have no time to lose. Start planting today."

It's planting time in America. Faulkner's old verities will take root again much sooner than the General's trees.

# IN REMEMBRANCE

## AN AMERICAN CREED[1]
### F. Forrester Church IV[2]

The fiftieth anniversary of the death of President Franklin D. Roosevelt was commemorated in various ways in 1995, including an observance at the Roosevelt Chapel in Warm Springs, Georgia, on April 9.

The chapel, located at the Roosevelt Warm Springs Institute for Rehabilitation, was founded by President Roosevelt for the treatment of polio patients. As a polio victim himself, Roosevelt regularly spent time in Warm Springs at the nearby Little White House, where he died on April 12, 1945. The chapel was where the President attended a service just before his sudden death. Today interdenominational services are held each Sunday in the chapel, with students and patients actively participating.

The Reverend F. Forrester Church of the Unitarian Church of All Souls in New York City was asked by the Franklin and Eleanor Roosevelt Institute to give the sermon at the fiftieth-year commemorative service in Warm Springs. The chapel service, which began at 11:00 a.m., included an organ prelude, hymns, scriptural readings, and prayers, as well as Dr. Church's sermon. The audience of approximately one hundred included ten members of the Roosevelt family, historian Arthur Schlesinger, and members of the Board of the Franklin and Eleanor Roosevelt Institute.

The ceremony was the first event in a four-day commemoration of the death of Franklin D. Roosevelt. Often activities included a two-day seminar with 258 participants and the presentation of Four Freedoms awards to Andrew Young, Jimmy Carter, Mary McGrory, Lane Kirkland, and Eliot Richardson.

Reverend Church later repeated his address, a sermon on April 30, 1995, at the Unitarian Church of All Souls in New York City.

[1]Delivered at a commemorative service, "Remembering Franklin Delano Roosevelt, 1882–1945" at the Roosevelt Chapel at the Roosevelt Warm Springs Institute for Rehabilitation in Warm Springs, Georgia on April 9, 1995.

[2]For biographical note see Appendix.

*Dr. Church's speech:* Let me open with a confession. I am not nearly as anxious as I should be at the prospect of preaching to this distinguished congregation on the fiftieth anniversary of Franklin Delano Roosevelt's death, even in the very chapel where he worshipped on the Sunday before he died. The reason for this is simple. My entire anxiety quotient is otherwise filled. It is filled by the much more daunting prospect of having to preach to my mother.

Have you ever tried preaching to your mother? It is an unnatural act. And not only do I have to preach to my mother, I also have to preach to my mother-in-law. If I were Al D'Amato I could at least lighten things up with a mother-in-law joke. But as Al will probably discover only after he gets remarried, mother-in-law jokes only work when one's mother-in-law is not present.

The nature of this occasion only compounds my particular anxiety. After all, my mother, Bethine Church, is the daughter of a New Deal Governor, Chase Clark of Idaho, and the wife of a United States Senator, Frank Church, who warmed his political toes on FDR's fireside chats. And my mother-in-law, Minna Buck, the first woman and first Democrat ever elected Family Court Judge in Syracuse, is nothing less than a living embodiment of Roosevelt values—Franklin and especially Eleanor Roosevelt values. Preaching to your mother and mother-in-law is hard enough without the additional burden of both knowing far more about your subject than you do.

Fortunately, I was raised to be presumptuous. Since my mother is in large measure responsible for this, any discomfort she may feel over the next twenty minutes is her own fault.

On the fiftieth anniversary of Franklin Delano Roosevelt's death, many of those who most respect his memory cannot help but feel a bit like Louis Carroll's *Alice*, suddenly diminished in size and power and awakening in an unfamiliar country, where insiders are out, outsiders in, and the rhetoric of right and wrong turned upside-down.

Not only would Newt Gingrich, the new queen of hearts, more appropriately be suited in clubs or diamonds, but, further to confound appearance and reality, of all our leaders it is he who most ostentatiously dons the Roosevelt mantle. "This is the year we rendezvous with our destiny." That's how he put it day before yesterday. FDR is his hero. That's what he says. It is enough to make the whole cemetery spin.

As for us liberals, at least the brave few who haven't gone back in the closet, something even curiouser appears to have happened. We have fallen through the looking glass only to emerge as arch defenders of the status quo. When it comes to preserving long-established government programs, regardless of the cost/benefit ratio, it is difficult to find any conservative more dogged than certain stalwarts of the liberal remnant.

Alice would certainly empathize with our disorientation.

"'Who are you?' the caterpillar asked.

'I—I hardly know, sir, just at present—at least I know who I was when I got up this morning, but I think I must have been changed several times since then.'

'What do you mean by that?' said the Caterpillar sternly. 'Explain yourself!'

'I can't explain myself, I'm afraid, sir,' said Alice, 'because I'm not myself, you see."

Six months into the post-Roosevelt era, with erstwhile conservatives storming the barricades and liberals who long have fashioned themselves progressive having to adjust to being "old-school"—plugging the dikes, trying to turn back the clocks—it sometimes appears that, unpracticed as a minority, the Democrats in Congress are taking too many classes with the mock-turtle. "'Once,' the mock-turtle said with a deep sigh, 'I was a real turtle.'" And what is taught in the mock-turtle's school? Well, "Reeling and Writhing, of course, to begin with, and then the different branches of Arithmetic—Ambition, Distraction, Uglification, and Derision." I have to admit, I sympathize. It is hardly surprising that Franklin Roosevelt's political children should evince all the classic symptoms of denial.

"Then it really has happened after all!" Alice says.

"'And now, who am I? I *will* remember, if I can! I'm determined to do it!"

But being determined didn't help her much, and all she could say, after a great deal of puzzling was "L, I know it begins with L.'"

In frustration, Alice then swore she should "never try to remember [her] name in the middle of an accident." Actually, there is no better time. Otherwise, as Alice almost did, we run the danger of drowning in our tears. Far better to staunch the tears of others. It is for this that our countrymen and women need us, not only to remember who we are as liberals, but, more importantly, to remember who we all ought to be as Americans.

The United States of America is a liberal democracy. It is the model for all other liberal democracies. The liberal impulse, both religious and political, shaped our country from its very inception. It informed the development of religious freedom, separation of church and state, equal protection under the law, freedom of speech and press, liberal education, and a generous-spirited social contract.

When the Carnegie Foundation asked Swedish economist and sociologist Gunnar Myrdal to do a study of America, he concluded that "America has had gifted conservative statesmen and national leaders . . . But with few exceptions, only the liberals have gone down in history as national heroes." Small wonder, for as the dictionary reminds us, liberal means free: worthy of a free person (as opposed to servile); free in bestowing; bountiful, generous, open-hearted; free from narrow prejudice; open-minded, candid; free from bigotry or unreasonable prejudice in favor of traditional opinions or established institutions; open to the reception of new ideas or proposals of reform; and, of political opinions, favorable to legal or administrative reforms tending in the direction of freedom or democracy.

Liberal means open-hearted, open-minded, and open-handed. It also means freedom: freedom from bondage; freedom for opportunity; and freedom with responsibility, especially toward our neighbor, whose rights and security are just as precious as our own. The American motto is *E pluribus unum*, out of many, one. When the narrow sympathies of some and the fear of others combine to mute this generous cry, we must give it new voice.

Since the term "doctrinaire liberal" is, by definition, an oxymoron, we are not likely to find that voice, at least not persuasively, in any set of specific programs, even those we are trying to preserve. We must instead recapture first the liberal spirit. I say recapture, because the liberal spirit, which is the American spirit, finds its most eloquent expression in symbols that have been ceded to or co-opted by the religious and political right.

Let's begin with the flag. It is one thing to wrap oneself in the flag, but those who do—and indeed those of us who reactively do not—might consider what it actually means to pledge allegiance to it: "I pledge allegiance to the flag of the United States of America, and to the republic for which it stands, one nation under God, indivisible, with liberty and justice for all."

This language encapsulates the true spirit of the American hope—*one nation under God, indivisible, with liberty and justice for all.* So how in the world have those of us who remain faithful to this spirit managed to get ourselves effectively branded as being anti-flag, anti-Bible, anti-American? Not simply by championing unpopular social programs in a selfish age: that's too convenient and self-flattering an answer. The real reason is this. We have relinquished the very symbols that speak most persuasively to the American heart. To make matters worse, we have ceded them to those who have their finger on its pulse but cannot feel its noble beat.

Listen to the American creed as it rings in Franklin Delano Roosevelt's words: "The basic things expected by our people of their political and economic systems are simple. They are equality of opportunity for youth and for others; jobs for those who can work; security for those who need it; the ending of special privilege for the few; the preservation of civil liberties for all; . . . Our nation has placed its destiny in the hands and hearts of its millions of free men and women, and its faith in freedom under the guidance of God. Freedom means the supremacy of human rights everywhere."

This, from his Four Freedoms Address, is a call not to American arms but to American hearts. It sets the tone for our gathering this week. Its refrain is the American creed: liberty and justice for all, one nation under God, indivisible. President Roosevelt's words chime in concert not only with our Pledge of Allegiance, but also with the scriptural passage our founders engraved on the Liberty Bell, taken from the Book of Leviticus: "Proclaim liberty throughout the land to all the inhabitants thereof."

The Liberty Bell, the Pledge of Allegiance to our nation and its flag: if one were looking for symbols to help explain the power Franklin Roosevelt's words and ideas held for the American people, one need look no further. Again and again, he sounded this prophetic chord, Biblical in cadence and tone, profoundly American in spirit.

Today, the same symbols—flag and Bible, the Liberty Bell, our country's founders, even Roosevelt himself—are invoked to inspire allegiance to a new, and radically different American revolution. Unlike Franklin Delano Roosevelt's vision, unlike the American creed, this new vision is apocalyptic, not prophetic. It appeals not to our faith, but to our fear; not to the better angels of our nature, but to the demons who drive our engines of recrimination. This new vision triumphs not by unifying all America in a brave, common endeavor, but by dividing us; not by encouraging us to conquer our fears, but by inciting us to conquer one another.

Nonetheless, this much must be said. Unlike the plaintive liberal efforts to shore up a tattered status quo, the leaders of the new American majority do offer what people hunger for in times of trouble: a clear, confident program for the future, made all the more powerful by tapping the deep vein of American loyalty to flag, Bible and family. Even should this vision prove to betray the very emblems it evokes, so long as these emblems remain identified with it, it will prevail. Such is their power, and certainly so, even when wrongfully used.

In these two respects, Newt Gingrich does in fact don the mantle of leadership that Franklin Roosevelt wore so effectively for so many years. And, at least for the time being, in these, the early days of Wonderland, those of us whose only answer is to frighten the electorate with the possible consequences of this new American contract, sound more like Hoover Republicans than Roosevelt Democrats. Remember, Franklin Roosevelt didn't say, "The only thing we have to fear is really very frightening." Had he done so, we would not be here on this occasion in this place, consecrating and seeking inspiration from his memory.

Things were far worse half a century ago than they are today. First the depression threatened to break the American spirit, then the Second World War taxed our unforged metal. We had far more reason for fear than we do now, more reason to succumb to temptations of neighborly hate. But Franklin Roosevelt didn't frighten people into voting for him. He inspired them to hearken to a higher call, not to his personal vision of freedom with equity, but to the transcendent ideals of liberty, justice and unity, the liberal religious, social and political ideals that our nation's founders codified as the American creed.

In 1932 at the Democratic National Convention, Franklin Roosevelt proclaimed that "The first obligation of government is the protection of the welfare and well-being, indeed the very existence, of its citizens." If the same words today are less convincing to the American electorate than hearing the Queen of Hearts run about her croquet court shouting "Off with their heads," during the interim something significant has happened. This speaks less, I think, to the intrinsic power of the liberal message than it does to the authority of its messengers. This authority has been diminished in two ways. We are now identified with a status quo that is clearly not working. And we seem to have forgotten how profoundly that message is grounded in the American creed.

"Will you tell me, please, which way I ought to go from here?" Alice asked the Cheshire cat.

"That depends a good deal on where you want to get to," the cat replied.

We know where we want to get to. It can perhaps best be summed up in one overarching question. How can we open the American heart once again to the plight of the poor? For Franklin Delano Roosevelt the poor were not a problem. In the deepest Christian and highest American sense, they present to the individual soul and larger community an opportunity. One nation, under God, indivisible, with liberty and justice for all: that is the American creed, and, as with all such faithfully grounded ideal aspirations, it is intrinsically inspiring. Deep in their hearts, influenced as they are both by Biblical and national ideals, the American people are ready to respond to this, even sacrifice for it.

The new American revolution fails to offer anything like the same moral, or spiritual challenge. All it offers is a way to take the poor off their neighbors' backs, and this, both effectively and perversely, in the name of God, flag and family.

So where do we go from here? The answer is not to stir up a sufficient amount of fear somehow to retain this or that old government program. Acting in the true spirit of Franklin Roosevelt, we must instead raise the common vision to something more commensurate to our treasured religious and societal ideals. Programs must and will follow, new experiments that will better approximate the fulfillment of those ideals than have our old ones, however well-intentioned. But first we must reclaim flag, Bible and family from their late captivity. Only then will we touch the American heart. Only then will we bid to restore its essential goodness.

When the Duchess said to Alice that love makes the world go round, Alice, in frustration at the rhetoric of Wonderland, whispered back, "Somebody said that it's done by everybody minding their own business!"

"'Ah, well! It means much the same thing,' said the Duchess, digging her sharp little chin into Alice's shoulder as she added, 'and the moral of that is—Take care of the sense, and the sounds will take care of themselves.'"

Of course, it is not the same thing. And sounds often carry further than sense does. This is why symbols are so powerful. Whoever claims them wields their power, both for good and for ill. And whoever yields them to those who would misrepresent their meaning must share in the consequences.

Alice escaped from Wonderland, which was only a dream after all, by calling the Queen's bluff.

"'Stuff and nonsense!' said Alice loudly.

'Hold your tongue!' said the Queen turning purple.

'I won't,' said Alice.

'Off with her head!' the Queen shouted at the top of her voice. Nobody moved.

'Who cares for you?' said Alice, (she had grown to her full size by this time.) 'You're nothing but a pack of cards.'"

We too can wake up, return to our full size, call things by their proper name, come back from beyond the looking glass. But first we have to remember who we are. We are liberals. And we are Americans. We have a creed to lift up and uphold. It is the American creed. It is written in the Bible's pages, in the Pledge of Allegiance, in the human heart. To do justly and love mercy. To love God and our neighbor as ourselves. To answer fear with faith.

In closing, I invite you to rise and recite it with me, our Pledge of Allegiance: "I pledge allegiance to the flag of the United States of America, and to the republic for which it stands, one nation, under God, indivisible, with liberty and justice for all."

---

## CLOSE YOUR EYES, AND LISTEN TO THE SILENT SCREAMS[1]
### Elie Wiesel[2]

---

Exactly fifty years after the liberation of the Nazi concentration camp at Auschwitz by the Soviet army, survivors and dignitaries gathered at the site of the camp to commemorate the event. Those attending the ceremonies included two monarchs, sixteen heads of state, two princes, press representatives, and a crowd of around five thousand including survivors of the camp and relatives of those killed. More than one and a half million persons had been exterminated at Auschwitz. More than ninety percent of those killed were Jews, although the victims also included Muslims, gypsies, and Poles.

[1]Delivered at a commemoration of the fiftieth anniversary of the liberation of the concentration camp at Auschwitz in Poland on January 27, 1995.

[2]For biographical note see Appendix.

The observance took place over two days, but the main ceremony was held on January 28, 1995, when the survivors and others attending were joined outside the camp by Polish President Lech Walesa; Speaker of the Israeli Parliament Sherach Weiss; and the writer Elie Wiesel, himself an Auschwitz survivor, and a Nobel peace laureate. The solemn procession, with many participants in tears, passed through the gates of the camp and walked to the Death Wall, the site of thousands of executions, where President Walesa delivered a speech.

Among those who addressed the crowd was Elie Wiesel. The setting for his speech was appropriately somber: the day had begun with a three minute siren blast—a signal for a prisoner escape—that pierced the bitter cold air. Many in the audience wore replicas of the striped uniforms once worn by the inmates, complete with the Star of David patches that identified Jews. After Jewish, Moslem, Roman Catholic, Orthodox Christian, Lutheran, and Calvinist prayers were heard, snow began to fall just as Wiesel commenced speaking.

*Mr. Wiesel's speech:* I speak to you as a man who 50 years and nine days ago had no name, no hope, no future and was known only by his number, A70713. I speak as a Jew, who has seen what humanity has done to itself by trying to exterminate an entire people and inflict suffering, humiliation and death on so many others.

And so all my life, underneath every word that I say or write, I repeat a prayer that you have heard earlier. For in this place of darkness and malediction, we can but stand and remember these stateless, faceless and nameless victims.

Presidents of states, friends, close your eyes; close your eyes and you will see what we have seen at night—endless nocturnal processions are converging here at night and here it is always night. Close your eyes and you will see that here heaven and earth are on fire.

Close your eyes, my friends, and listen, listen to the silent screams of terrified mothers, listen to the prayers of anguished old men and women, listen to the tears of children, Jewish children, beautiful looking girls among them, with golden hair, whose vulnerable tenderness never left me.

Look and listen as the victims quietly walk towards dark flames so gigantic that the planet itself seemed in danger.

All these men, women and children came from everywhere. We had a feeling that it was a gathering of exiles drawn by death, by death alone, as if they had wanted to come home—but home was death.

And so what else can we say but the prayer. I also speak on behalf of the President of the United States and the people of America and all those who have seen what we have seen.

The president asked me to read a message. I shall only read excerpts.

He said: "We remember the victims. Each was a person in the image of God, a son or daughter, a mother or father, a wife or a husband, a sister or brother, a friend or neighbour, rich or poor . . ."

And the president said: "The Jewish people were singled out for destruction during the Holocaust and shoulder history's heaviest burden." I say in this kingdom of darkness there were many people. People who came from all the occupied lands of Europe. And then there were the gypsies, the Poles and the Czechs.

It is true that not all the victims were Jews. But all the Jews were victims.

So look and listen, close your eyes and listen and open your hearts and listen to the questions we asked ourselves then. What happened here? When we came, we wondered: what was the meaning of it all?

The killers killed, the victims died and the world was the world and everything else was going on, life as usual. In the towns nearby, what happened? In the lands nearby, what happened?

Life was going on. Where God's creation was condemned to blasphemy by the killers and their accomplices. Now and then we ask ourselves, what is the lesson? The lesson is, I believe, not to yield to hatred, to fight fanaticism and the violence and the terror. Let there be a stop to violence and bloodshed in those lands where people still kill one another.

Let the terrorism stop in the Holy Land. Enough! Where else can we say to the world, "Remember the morality of the human condition," if not here?

Weep for the children, our Father in heaven. For they were deprived of their right to be buried . . . All will be remembered.

All of us must remember. There must be a future . . . I do not want the next generation, our children's generation, I do not want my past to become their future.

That is why we are here, in this place of darkness and mortality, as we all close our eyes and open our hearts to human memory.

# APPENDIX

## BIOGRAPHICAL NOTES

ALEXANDER, JANE, (1939– ). Born, Boston, Massachusetts; student, Sarah Lawrence College, 1957–59, University of Edinburgh, 1959–60; independent TV, film, and theatrical actress, 1962– ; Chairman National Endowment of the Acts, 1993– ; appeared in production, Charles Playhouse, Boston, 1964–65, Arena Stage, Washington, 1965–68, 70– , American Shakespeare Festival, Broadway production, 1968–1993; member Women's Action for New Directions (advisory board of directors, 1981–88); N.Y. Sociological Society/Wildlife Conservation Society (advisory board of directors, 1984–93); Film Forum (board of directors, 1985–90); National Stroke Association (advisory board of directors, 1985–93, advisory board, 1990– ); Achievement in Dramatic Arts Award, St. Botolph Club, 1979; Israel Cultural Award, 1982; Western Heritage Wrangler Award, 1985; Helen Caldicott Leadership Award, 1984; Living Legacy Award, Women's International Center, San Diego, 1988; Environmental Leadership Award, Eco-Expo, 1991; Muse Award, N.Y. Women in film, 1993; named to Theatre Hall of Fame, 1994; author, (with Greta Jacobs) *The Bluefish Cookbook*, 4 editions, 1979–92; translator, (with Sam Engelstad) *The Master Builder* (Henrik Ibsen), 1978; Tony Award, 1969, nominated for several Tony Awards, Emmy Awards, and Academy Awards.

CHURCH, FRANK FORRESTER IV (1948– ). Born, Boise, Idaho; B.A., with distinction, Stanford University, 1970; M.Div., magna cum laude, Harvard University, 1974, Ph.D., 1978; minister, Unitarian Church of All Souls, New York City, 1978– ; Montgomery Fellow and visiting professor, Dartmouth College, 1989; author and editor of more than twenty books, including *Father and Son: A Personal Biography of Senator Frank Church of Idaho by His Son*, 1985, *The Devil and Dr. Church*, 1986, *Entertaining Angels*, 1987, *The Essential Tillich*, 1987, *The Seven Deadly Virtues*, 1989, *God and Other Famous Liberals: Reclaiming the Politics of America*, 1992; articles on New Testament studies, the history of early Christianity, the history of liberal religion, and contemporary theological topics.

CLINTON, BILL (WILLIAM JEFFERSON) (1946– ). Born, Hope, Arkansas; B.S., Georgetown University, 1968; Rhodes Scholar, Oxford University, 1968–70; J.D., Yale University, 1973; professor, University of Arkansas Law School, 1973–76; Attorney General of Arkansas, 1977–79; Governor of Arkansas, 1979–81, 1983–92; counsel, Wright, Lindsey, & Jennings, Little Rock, 1981–82; chairman, Education Commission of the States, 1986–87; chairman, Democratic Leadership Council, 1990–91; president of the United States, 1993– .

Cuomo, Mario Matthew (1932– ). Born, Queens County, New York; B.A., St. John's College, 1953; LL.B., St. John's University, 1956; admitted to New York Bar, 1956, U.S. Supreme Court Bar, 1960; confidential legal assistant to judge New York State Court of Appeals, 1956–58; associate firm Corner, Wiesbrod, Froeb and Charles, Brooklyn, 1958–63, partner 1963–75; secretary of state State of New York, 1975–79; lieutenant governor, 1979–82, governor, 1983– ; faculty, St. John's University School of Law, 1963–73; counsel to community groups including Corona Homeowners, 1966–72; charter member 1st Ecumenical Community of Christians and Jews for Brooklyn and Queens, 1965; member, ABA, New York State, Brooklyn, Nassau, and Queens County Bar Associations, Association Bar City New York, American Judicature Society, St. John's University Alumni Federation (chairman, board, 1970–72), Catholic Lawyers Guild of Queens County (president, 1966–67), Skull and Circle; recipient, Rapalla Award Columbia Lawyers Association, 1976, Dante medal Italian Government-American Association of Teachers of Italian, 1975, silver medallion Columbia Coalition, 1976, Public Administrator Award C. W. Post College, 1977; author, *Forest Hills Diary: The Crisis of Low-Income Housing*, 1974, *Diaries of Mario M. Cuomo: The Campaign for Governor*, 1984; contributor of articles to legal publications. (See also *Current Biography*, August 1983.)

Eitzen, David Stanley (1934– ). Born, Glendale, California; B.A., Bethel College, 1956; M.S., Emporia State University, 1962; M.A., University of Kansas, 1966, Ph.D., 1968; recreational therapist, Menninger Foundation, 1956–58; teacher, Galva High School (Kansas), 1958–60, Turner High School (Kansas), 1960–65; assistant professor, University of Kansas, 1968–72, associate professor, 1972–74; professor, Colorado State University, 1974– ; president, North American Society for the Sociology of Sport, 1986–87; executive council, Western Social Science Association, 1978–84; chair, Theory Division, Society for the Study of Social Problems, 1986–88; executive council, section on Undergraduate Education, American Sociological Association, 1987–90; member, International Sociological Association, American Sociological Association, Midwest Sociological Society, Society for the Study of Social Problems, Western Social Science Association, International Committee for the Sociology of Sport, North American Society for the Sociology of Sport, American Society of Criminology; Distinguished Alumnus Award, Emporia State University, 1989; special recognition for contributions to the Western Social Science Association on its 30th Anniversary, 1988; Excellence in Research and Creativity, College of Arts, Humanities and Social Sciences, Colorado State University, 1988; N.D.E.A. Fellow, 1965–67; editor, *The Social Science Journal*, 1978–84; author, *Social Structure and Social Problems in America*, 1974, *Sociology of North American Sport* (with George H. Sage), 1978, *In Conflict and Order*, 1978, *Sport in Contemporary America* (ed.), 1979, *Social Problems*, 1980, *Elite Deviance* (with David R. Simon), 1982, *Criminology* (with Doug A. Timmer), 1985, *Diversity in American Families* (with Maxine Baca Zinn), 1987, *Crime in the Streets and Crime in the Suites* (ed., with Doug A. Timmer), 1989, *The Reshaping of America* (ed., with Maxine Baca Zinn),

1989, and *Society's Problems* (ed.), 1989; over 100 articles in professional journals and chapters in scholarly books.

GINGRICH, NEWTON LEROY (1943– ). Born, Harrisburg, Pennsylvania; B.A., Emory University, 1965; M.A., Tulane University, 1968, Ph.D., 1971; Faculty West Georgia College, 1970–78; assistant professor, West Georgia College until 1978; member 96th–103rd Congresses 1989–92; House of Representatives whip 96th–102nd Congresses 1989– : general chairman GOPAC; co-founder Conservative Opportunity Soc., congressional military caucus; space caucus; member joint committee on printing; house administration committee, co-chairman Leader's Task Force on Health; author, (with Marianne Gingrich) *Window of Opportunity.*

GOULD, WILLIAM BENJAMIN IV (1930– ). A.B. University of Rhode Island, 1958, LL.B. Cornell University, 1961, post-graduate, London School of Economics, 1962–63, LL.B. (honorary) University of Rhode Island, 1986; assistant general counsel, Y.A.W., A.F.L.-c.i.o., K96k–92, National Labor Relations Board, Washington, D.C., 1963–65; professor, Wayne State University, 1968–71; professor, Stanford University Law School, 1971– ; chairman, National Labor Relations Board, 1994– ; visiting scholar, Cambridge University, 1975, University of Tokyo, 1975, Australian National University, 1983, European University of Florence, Italy, 1988, and University of Witwatersand, 1991.

GRONBECK, BRUCE ELLIOTT, (1941– ). Born, Bertha, Minnesota; B.A., Concordia College, 1963; M.A., University of Iowa, 1966, Ph.D., 1970; lecturer, University of Michigan, 1967–70, assistant professor, 1970–73; associate professor, University of Iowa, 1973–80; project director, Center for Research & Teaching Giant, University of Michigan, 1967–68; project administrator, Carnegie Corporation Grant, 1971–73; co-director, Bicentennial Film Project, NEH, 1972–73; president, Central States Speech Association, 1977–78; president, Speech Communication Association, 1993.

HYDE, HENRY JOHN, (1924– ). Born, Chicago, Illinois; student, Duke University, 1943–44; B.S., Georgetown University, 1946; J.D., Loyola University, 1949; served with United States Navy, 1944–46; member, Illinois General Assembly, 1967–74; 94th–103rd Congresses from 6th Illinois district, 1975– ; member Foreign Affairs committee, subcommittee International Operations, judicial committee, subcommittee on civil and constitutional rights; Chicago Bar Association.

JORDAN, VERNON E., JR. (1935– ). Born, Atlanta, Georgia; B.A., De-Pauw University, 1957; first prize, Indiana Interstate Oratorical Contest, sophomore year; J.D., Howard University, 1960; honorary degrees from thirty institutions; circuit vice-president of American Law Students Association while at Howard University; helped to desegregate the University of Georgia; clerk in law office of civil rights attorney Donald Hollowell; field secretary, NAACP, Georgia branch, 1952; set up law partnership in Arkansas with another civil rights lawyer, Wiley A. Barnton, 1964; director, Voter Education Project for the Southern Regional Council, 1964–68;

executive director, United Negro College Fund, 1970–72; director, National Urban League, January 1972–81; partner, Atkin, Gump, Strauss, Hauer and Feld law firm, Washington, D.C., 1981– ; member, Arkansas and Georgia Bar Associations, U.S. Supreme Court Bar, American Bar Association, Common Cause, Rockefeller Foundation, Twentieth Century Fund, other service organizations; has held fellowships at Harvard University's Institute of Politics, the John F. Kennedy School of Government, and the Metropolitan Applied Research Center; serves on boards of several corporations. (See also *Current Biography*, February 1972.)

KENNAN, GEORGE FROST (1904– ). Born, Milwaukee, Wisconsin; A.B., Princeton University, 1925, LL.D. (honorary) 1956; additional honorary degrees from 24 universities; foreign service positions in Moscow, Vienna, Prague, Berlin, Lisbon, London, Hamburg, Finland, 1927–1952; ambassador to USSR, 1952, and to Yugoslavia, 1961–1963; Bancroft Prize, National Book Award (twice), Albert Einstein Peace Prize, Grenville Clark Prize, and other prizes; author of 15 books on foreign policy.

KENNEDY, EDWARD MOORE (1932– ). Born, Boston, Massachusetts; A.B., Harvard University, 1956; student, International Law School, The Hague, The Netherlands, 1958; LL.B., University of Virginia, 1959; honorary degrees, thirteen institutions; admitted, Massachusetts Bar, 1959; assistant district attorney, Suffolk County, Massachusetts, 1961–62; U.S. senator, Massachusetts, 1962– ; former assistant majority leader, U.S. Senate; chairman, judiciary committee, 1979–81; member, labor and human resources committee, 1981– ; president, Joseph P. Kennedy Jr. Foundation, 1961– ; member, board of trustees, universities, hospitals, libraries, the Boston Symphony, John F. Kennedy Center for the Performing Arts, and Robert F. Kennedy Memorial Foundation; named one of ten outstanding young men in United States by Junior Chamber of Commerce, 1967; author, *Decisions for a Decade*, 1968, *In Critical Condition: The Crisis in America's Health Care*, 1972, *Our Day and Generation*, 1979, *Freeze: How You Can Help Prevent Nuclear War* (with Mark O. Hatfield), 1979. (See also *Current Biography*, 1978.)

ROONEY, ANDREW AITKEN, (1919– ). Born, Albany, New York; student, Colgate University, 1942; writer-producer CBS-TV News, 1959– ; newspaper columnist Tribune Co. Syndicate, 1979– ; author, (with O. C. Hutton) *Air Gunner*, 1944, *The Story of Stars and Stripes*, 1946, *Conquerors' Peace*, 1947, *The Fortunes of War*, 1962, *A Few Minutes with Andy Rooney*, 1981, *And More By Andy Rooney*, 1982, *Pieces of My Mind*, 1984, *Word for Word*, 1986, *Not That You Asked*, 1989, *Sweet and Sour*, 1992; TV programs include *An Essay on War, Mr. Rooney goes to Washington, Mr. Rooney goes to Dinner;* regular commentator-essayist, *60 Minutes*, 1978– ; served with AUS, 1941–45, decorated Air medal, Bronze Star; recipient awards for best written TV documentary, Writers Guild Am., 1966, 68, 71, 75, 76, Emmy awards, 1968, 78, 81, 82.

SCHLESINGER, JAMES RODNEY (1929– ). Born, New York City; A.B. Harvard University, 1950, A.M., 1952, Ph.D., 1956; assistant and associate professor, University of Virginia, 1955–1963; assistant director, Office of

Management and Budget, 1970–1971; director, Central Intelligence Agency, 1973; U.S. Secretary of Defense, 1973–1975; assistant Secretary of Department of Energy, 1977–1979; counselor, Center for Strategic Studies, Georgetown University, 1979– ; author, *The Political Economy of National Security, 1960, America at Century's End,* 1989, co-author, *Issues in Defense Economics,* 1967.

VALENTI, JACK JOSEPH (1921– ). Born, Houston, Texas; B.A., University of Houston, 1946, M.B.A., Harvard University, 1948; co-founder and formerly executive vice-president *Weekly and Valenti, Inc.,* 1952–1963; special assistant to President Lyndon B. Johnson, 1963–1966; president and chief executive office, Motion Picture Association of America, 1966– ; author, *Bitter Taste of Glory,* 1971, *A Human President,* 1976, *Speak Up With Confidence: How to Prepare and Deliver an Effective Speech,* 1982, *Protect and Defend,* 1992.

WIESEL, ELIE(ZER) (1928– ). Born, Sighet, Transylvania; came to U.S., 1956, naturalized; attended Sorbonne, University of Paris, 1947–50; honorary degrees, twenty-nine institutions; foreign correspondent at various times for *Yedioth Ahronoth,* Tel Aviv, Israel, *L'Arche,* Paris, France, and *Jewish Daily Forward,* New York City, 1949– ; professor, City College of the City University of New York, New York City, 1972–76; Andrew Mellon Professor in the Humanities, Boston University, Boston, Massachusetts, 1976– ; Henry Luce Visiting Scholar, Yale University, New Haven, Connecticut; chairman, U.S. President's Commission on the Holocaust, U.S. Holocaust Memorial Council; board of directors, National Committee on American Foreign Policy, Hebrew Arts School, Humanitas, International Rescue Committee; board of governors, Oxford Center for Postgraduate Hebrew Studies, Ben-Gurion University of the Negev, Haifa University, Tel-Aviv University; colleague, Cathedral of St. John the Divine; member, Amnesty International; Writers and Artists for Peace in the Middle East; Phi Beta Kappa; honorary chairman, National Jewish Resource Center; recipient, Prix Rivarol, 1964, Jewish Heritage Award, Haifa University, 1965, Remembrance Award, 1965, Prix Medicis, 1968, Prix Bordin French Academy, 1972, Eleanor Roosevelt Memorial Award, New York United Jewish Appeal, 1972, Martin Luther King, Jr. Medallion, City College of the City University of New York, 1973, Faculty Distinguished Scholar Award, Hofstra University, 1973–74, Jewish Heritage Award, B'Nai B'rith, Avoda Award, Jewish Teachers Association, Humanitarian Award, B'rith Sholom, Jabotinsky Medal, State of Israel, International Literature Prize for Peace, Royal Academy, Belgium, 1983, Congressional Gold Medal, 1984, Remembrance Award, Israel Bonds, 1985, Anne Frank Award, 1985; Jacob Javits Humanitarian Award, Freedom Cup Womens League Israel, Nobel Peace Prize, Medal of Liberty Award Statue of Liberty Presentation, 1986, Profiles of Courage Award, B'Nai B'rith, Golda Meir Humanitarian Award, 1987, Presidential Medal Hofstra University, Human Rights Law award International Human Rights Law Group, 1988; fellow, Jewish Academy of Arts and Sciences, Timothy Dwight College, Yale University; author of twenty-three books including *Night,* 1960, *Dawn,* 1961, *The Accident,* 1962, *A Beggar in Jerusalem,* 1970,

*Souls on Fire,* 1972, *The Fifth Son,* 1985, *Against Silence,* 1985, *A Song for Hope,* 1987, *The Nobel Speech,* 1987, *Tempete Twilight,* 1988, *The Six Days of Destruction,* 1988, *From the Kingdom of Memory,* 1990; editorial boards of *Midstream, Religion and Literature, Sh'ma: Journal of Responsibility;* (See also *Current Biography,* 1986.)

# CUMULATIVE SPEAKER INDEX

## 1990–1995

A cumulative author index to the volumes of *Representative American Speeches* for the years 1937–1938 through 1959–1960 appears in the 1959–1960 volume, for the years 1960–1961 through 1969–1970 in the 1969–1970 volume, for the years 1970–1971 through 1979–1980 in the 1979–1980 volume, and for the years 1980–1981 through 1989–1990 in the 1989–1990 volume.

Abbas, Mahmoud, 1993–94, 100–110, Building Peace in the Middle East

Archambault, David, 1992–93, 71–78, Whither the American Indian: Columbus Plus 500 Years?

Alexander, Jane, 1994–95, 143–149, The Arts and Education

Arafat, Yasir, 1993–94, 108–109, Building Peace in the Middle East

Bickel, K. R., 1991–92, 140–146, Forgive Mankind's Atrocities

Billington, J. H., 1991–92, 9–20, The Rebirth of Russia; 1993–94, 168–174, Preparing for Our Greatest Challenge

Bok, Derek, 1991–92, 106–116, The Social Responsibilities of American Universities

Bradley, W. W. (Bill), 1991–92, 127–139, Race and the American City; 1993–94, 27–38, An Economic Security Platform

Branch, Taylor, 1992–93, 55–65, Democracy in an Age of Denial

Bush, Barbara, 1990–91, 161–188, Choices and Change

Bush, G. H. W., 1990–91, 37–43, Operation Desert Storm, 43–48, The War is Over: A Framework for Peace; 1991–92, 91–98, America 2000: An Education Strategy; 1992–93, 15–24, Farewell Address: American Intervention

Cheney, L. V., 1991–92, 116–126, Political Correctness and Beyond

Christopher, Warren, 1992–93, 44–54, American Foreign Policy in a New Age

Church, F. F., IV, 1992–93, 65–70, Shall We Overcome?; 1994–95, 71–78, Fear and Terror, 156–163, An American Creed

Clinton, Hillary Rodham, 1993–94, 48–62, Improving Health Care

Clinton, W. J. (Bill), 1991–92, 49–60, The New Covenant: Responsibility and Rebuilding the American Community; 1992–93, 9–14, Inaugural Address, 24–35, State of the Union Address; 1993–94, 9–26, Inaugural Address, 100–110, Building Peace in the Middle East; 1994–95, 9–30, State of the Union

Colson, C. W., 1991–92, 21–36, The Problem of Ethics; 1993–94, 63–72, The Enduring Revolution

Cuomo, Mario M., 1994–95, 50–65, A Farewell to Public Office

D'Alemberte, Talbot, 1991–92, 79–90, Civil Justice Reform

Danforth, John, 1992–93, 118–123, The Meaning of the Holocaust to Christians

Dinkins, D. N., 1990–91, 129–143, In Praise of Cities

Edelman, M. W., 1990–91, 151–161, The Lessons of Life

Edwards, E. W., 1991–92, 60–70, Inaugural Address

Eitzen, D. S., 1991–93, 91–97, National Security: Children, Crime, and Cities; 1994–95, 78–87, Violent Crime: Myths, Facts, and Solutions

Ford, G. R., 1990–91, 184–196, Dwight D. Eisenhower: A Remembrance and Rededication

Frohnmayer, J. E., 1990–91, 143–150, Community and the Arts, 1991–92, 147–157, Free Expression and Human Rights

Geiger, K. B., 1991–92, 98–106, A Bill of Rights for Children

Gerbner, George, 1991–92, 169–181, Instant History in the Persian Gulf: Like Going to a Movie

Gerety, Tom, 1992–93, 98–102, Saving Our Cities

Gingrich, Newton L., 1994–95, 30–40, A Contract with America

Gore, Albert, Jr., 1993–94, 82–87, Days of Remembrance

Gronbeck, Bruce E., 1994–95, 95–110, Electric Rhetoric: The Transformation of American Political Talk

Gould, William B., IV, 1994–95, 111–120, Lincoln, Labor, and the Black Military

Hackney, Sheldon, 1993–94, 140–147, Beyond the Cultural Wars

Haiman, F. S., 1990–91, 93–105, Majorities versus the First Amendment

Hilliard, William A., 1993–94, 134–139, Values Deserving Our Attention

Hyde, Henry J., 1994–95, 65–70, Congressional Term Limits

Jordan, Barbara, 1992–93, 111–117, The Arts and the American Dream

Jordan, Vernon E., Jr., 1994–95, 120–127, The Struggle Is Not Over

Kagan, Donald, 1990–91, 167–174, E. Pluribus Unum

Kennedy, Edward M., 1994–95, 41–50, Commitment to Values

Kennan, George F., 1994–95, 128–132, Defining American Foreign Policy

Kindred, D. A., 1991–92, 182–192, Ninety Feet is Perfection

Lay, D. P., 1990–91, 105–111, Our Justice System, So-Called

Lewis, Bernard, 1990–91, 7–24, Western Civilization: A View from the East

Linowitz, Sol M., 1993–94, 175–178, Educating for National Security

Lyman, P. N., 1990–91, 74–81, Refugees in the 1990s

Mann, J. M., 1990–91, 82–92, Global AIDS: Revolution, Paradigm and Solidarity

Mathews, J. T., 1990–91, 57–61, Man and Nature: The Future of Global Environment

McCullough, David, 1993–94, 148–160, A Sense of Proportion

Meneilly, Robert, 1993–94, 74–81, The Dangers of Religion

Minow, N. M., 1990–91, 111–125, Communication in Medicine, 1991–92, 158–169, How Vast the Wasteland Now?

Mitrovich, G. S., 1991–92, 36–48, Money and the Politics of Betrayal

Moseley-Braun, Carol, 1992–93, 123–127, Tribute to Thurgood Marshall, 1993–94, 88–99, Getting Beyond Racism

Nolan, Joseph, 1992–93, 35–43, The Presidency and Public Opinion

Peres, Shimon, 1993–94, 103–105, Building Peace in the Middle East

Perot, H. R., 1990–91, 25–36, First Commit the Nation, Then Commit the Troops

Powell, Colin, 1993–94, 179–192, American Military Leadership

Quayle, J. D., 1991–92, 71–79, The Most Litigious Society in the World

Rabin, Yitzhak, 1993–94, 106–108, Building Peace in the Middle East

Rather, Dan, 1993–94, 123–133, Call to Courage

Rawlings, H. R. III, 1992–93, 82–91, The University and the Public

Redford, Robert, 1990–91, 49–57, Saving the Environment

Reedy, G. E., 1990–91, 174–183, Changing Perspectives in Education

Reno, Janet, 1993–94, 39–47, Combatting Crime

Roberts, Eugene L., Jr., 1993–94, 161–167, Writing for the Reader

Rooney, Andrew A., 1994–95, 88–95, Television News Reporting

Sagan, Carl, 1992–93, 78–81, A Thousand Thomas Jeffersons

Schlesinger, James R., 1994–95, 132–142, American Leadership, Isolationism, and Unilateralism

Simon, Paul, 1993–94, 111–122, Violence on Television and Film: An Appeal for Responsibility

Tobias, R. L., 1992–93, 102–110, In Today Walks Tomorrow

Valenti, Jack J., 1994–95, 149–155, William Faulkner's Old Verities: It's Planting Time in America

Wattleton, Faye, 1990–91, 125–128, Reproductive Freedom: Fundamental to All Human Rights

Wiesel, Elie, 1990–91, 69–73, The Shame of Hunger; 1994–95, 163–165, Close Your Eyes and Listen to the Silent Screams

# INDEX TO VOLUME 67 (1995)
# BY SUBJECT

*Criminal Sentencing (67:1)*
*Suicide (67:2)*
*Genetics and Society (67:3)*
*Gambling (67:4)*
*The Information Revolution (67:5)*
*Representative American Speeches (67:6)*

**ABORTION**
### Moral and Religious Aspects
Coming soon: your neighborhood T.S.C. P. J. Bernardi. *America* Ap. 30, '94. **67:2**

**ABUSED CHILDREN**
### Psychology
Verbal and physical abuse as stressors in the lives of lesbian, gay male, and bisexual youths. R. C. Savin-Williams. *Journal of Consulting and Clinical Psychology* Ap.'94. **67:2**

**ADOLESCENT PSYCHOLOGY**
Verbal and physical abuse as stressors in the lives of lesbian, gay male, and bisexual youths. R. C. Savin-Williams. *Journal of Consulting and Clinical Psychology* Ap. '94. **67:2**

**AGED PRISONERS**
A solution to prison overcrowding. J. Turley. *USA Today* N. '92. **67:1**

**AGRICULTURAL RESEARCH**
### Developing Countries
Can biotech put bread on third world tables? J. E. Ellis. *Business Week* D. 14, '92. **67:3**

Genetic engineering in food biotechnology. H. Dorenburg and C. Lang-Hinrichs. *Chemistry & Industry* Jl. 4, '94. **67:3**

**AIDS**
### Therapy
Genetic attacks on AIDS readied. G. Kolata. *New York Times* My. 31, '94. **67:3**

**ART**
The arts and education. J. Alexander. Speech delivered My. 20, '94. **67:6**

**ASSISTED SUICIDE**
Coming soon: your neighborhood T.S.C. P. J. Bernardi. *America* Ap. 30, '94. **67:2**

The Oregon trail to death. C. S. Campbell. *Commonweal* Ag. 19, '94. **67:2**

Rx for death. N. R. Gibbs. *Time* My. 31, '93. **67:2**

Death with dignity. W. M. McCord. *The Humanist* Ja./F. '93. **67:2**

Death on trial. J. P. Shapiro. *U.S. News & World Report* Ap. 25, '94. **67:2**

Close your eyes and listen to the silent screams. E. Wiesel. *New York Times* Ja. 20, '95. **67:6**

**BIOENGINEERED FOODS**

Can biotech put bread on third world tables? J. E. Ellis. *Business Week* D. 14, '92. **67:3**

The coming of the high-tech harvest. P. Weintraub. *Audubon* Jl./Ag.'92. **67:3**

**BLACK ON BLACK CRIME**

Action Jackson. H. Rosin. *The New Republic* Mr. 21, '94. **67:1**

**BLACKS**
**Boys**

Most dangerous and endangered. R. Tetzeli. *Fortune* Ag. 10, '92. **67:1**
**Crime**

No justice, no peace. R. Szykowny. *The Humanist* Ja./F.'94. **67:1**

Witness to another execution. S. Blaustein. *Harper's* My. '94. **67:1**
**Military**

Lincoln, labor, and the black military: the legacy provided. W. B. Gould IV. Speech delivered F. 11, '95. **67:6**
**Rights and Influence**

The struggle is not over. V. E. Jordan Jr. Speech delivered My. 14, '94. **67:6**

**CALIFORNIA YOUTH AUTHORITY**
**About**

California's teen gangs. D. Foote. *Newsweek* Jl. 4, '94. **67:1**

**CAPITAL PUNISHMENT**

Not in my name. B. Dority. *The Humanist* Mr./Ap. '93. **67:1**

Catholics and the death penalty. R. F. Drinan. *America* Je. 18–25, '94. **67:1**

The Supreme Court and capital punishment. C. F. Murphy. *USA Today* Mr. '93. **67:1**

You don't always get Perry Mason. R. Lacayo. *Time* Je. 1, '92. **67:1**

**CASINOS**

Casino craze. P. Hellman. *Travel Holiday* Mr. '94. **67:4**

Tricks of the trade. J. Popkin. *U.S. News & World Report* Mr. 14, '94. **67:4**

**CATHOLIC CHURCH**
**United States**

Catholics and the death penalty. R. F. Drinan. *America* Je. 18–25, '94. **67:1**

**CHILDREN OF EXECUTIVES**

Why grade "A" execs get an "F" as parents. B. O'Reilly. *Fortune* Ja. 1, '90.
    **67:2**

**COBAIN, KURT**
### About
Obituary. A. DeCurtis. *Rolling Stone* Je. 2, '94. **67:2**

**COMPULSIVE GAMBLING**

Compulsive gambling. H. R. Lesieur. *Society* My./Je. '92. **67:4**

Refuting the myths of compulsive gambling. R. E. Vatz and L. S. Wein-
    berg. *USA Today* N.'93. **67:4**

**COMPUTER**
### Civilization
Breaking the box. G. F. Gilder. *National Review* Ag. 15, '94. **67:5**
### Crime
Policing cyberspace. V. Sussman. *U.S. News & World Report* Ja. 23, '95.
    **67:5**

Wire pirates. P. Wallich. *Scientific American* Mr.'94. **67:5**
### Pornography
The naked city. J. Zipperer. *Christian Today* S. 12, '94. **67:5**
### Television
Breaking the box. G. F. Gilder. *National Review* Ag. 15, '94. **67:5**
### Women
Sex & the super-highway. B. Fryer. *Working Woman* Ap. '94. **67:5**

**CONGRESS**
### Amendments
Congressional term limits. H. J. Hyde. Speech delivered Mr. 29, '95. **67:6**

**COOK, ANTHONY**
### About
Witness to another execution. S. Blaustein. *Harper's* My. '94. **67:1**

**CRIME and CRIMINALS**
### Economic Aspects
Lock 'em up can't possibly cut crime much. D. C. Anderson. *New York
    Times* Je. 12, '94. **67:1**

The economics of crime. M. J. Mandel. and P. Magnusson. *Business Week*
    D. 13, '93. **67:1**
### Prevention
Violent crime: myths, facts, and solutions. D. S. Eitzen. *Vital Speeches of
    the Day* My. 15, '95. **67:6**
### Sentences
A cold-eyed look at crime. T. Gest and G. Witkin. *U.S. News & World
    Report* Je. 27, '94. **67:1**

**CRIMINAL JUSTICE, ADMINISTRATION of**

 . . . and throw away the key. J. Smolowe. *Time* F. 7, '94. **67:1**

No justice, no peace. R. Szykowny. *The Humanist* Ja./F.'94. **67:1**
### Texas
Witness to another execution. S. Blaustein. *Harper's* My. '94. **67:1**
## CYSTIC FIBROSIS
### Diagnosis
To test or not to test? L. Roberts. *Science* Ja. 5, '90. **67:3**
## DEATH
Dead complicated. E. Rosenthal. *Discover* O. '92. **67:2**
Planning to die. J. H. Guillemin. *Society* Jl./Ag. '92. **67:2**
## DEATH PENALTY
Catholics and the death penalty. R. F. Drinan. *America* Je. 18-25, '94. **67:1**
Not in my name. B. Dority. *The Humanist* Mr./Ap. '93. **67:1**
## DEMOCRACY
Democracy on-line. J. H. Snider. *The Futurist* S./O. '94. **67:5**
## DEMOCRATIC PARTY
### About
Commitment to values. E. M. Kennedy. Speech delivered Ja. 11, '95. **67:6**
## EDUCATION
The arts and education. J. Alexander. Speech delivered My. 20, '94. **67:6**
William Faulkner's old verities: it's planting time in America. J. J. Valenti. Speech delivered Ja. 24, '95. **67:6**
## ELECTRONIC MAIL SYSTEMS
### Security Measures
Wire pirates. P. Wallich. *Scientific American* Mr. '94. **67:5**
### Electronic Shopping
Will the information superhighway be the death of retailing? S. Sherman. *Fortune* Ap. 18, '94. **67:5**
### Electronic Town Meetings
Democracy on-line. J. H. Snider. *The Futurist* S./O. '94. **67:5**
### Electronics in Crime Prevention
Walking prisons: the developing technology of electronic controls. M. Winkler. *The Futurist* Jl./Ag. '93. **67:1**
## EUTHANASIA
Coming soon: your neighborhood T.S.C. P. J. Bernardi. *America* Ap. 30, '94. **67:2**
Death news. A. Fadiman. *Harper's* Ap. '94. **67:2**
Death with dignity. W. M. McCord. *The Humanist* Ja./F. '93. **67:2**
Death on trial. J. P. Shapiro. *U.S. News & World Report* Ap. 25, '94. **67:2**
## EXECUTIVES' FAMILIES
Why grade "A" execs get an "F" as parents. B. O'Reilly. *Fortune* Ja. 1, '90. **67:2**

**FOOD SUPPLY**
**Developing Countries**
Can biotech put bread on third world tables? J. E. Ellis. *Business Week* D. 14, '92. **67:3**

American killers are getting younger. J. A. Fox and G. L. Pierce. *USA Today* Ja. '94. **67:1**

**FOREIGN POLICY**
Defining American foreign policy. G. F. Kennan. Speech delivered O. 17, '94. **67:6**

American leadership, isolationism, and unilateralism. J. R. Schlesinger. Speech delivered Ap. 6, '95. **67:6**

**FOXWOODS HIGH STAKES BINGO & CASINO**
**About**
Revenge of the Indians. K. I. Eisler. *The Washingtonian* Ag. '93. **67:4**

Watching dad gamble. P. Jordan. *Yankee* Jl. '93. **67:5**

**GAMBLING**
Behind the lights, casino burnout. J. Nordheimer. *New York Times* Ag. 5, '94. **67:4**

Casino craze. P. Hellman. *Travel Holiday* Mr.'94. **67:4**

Compulsive gambling. H. R. Lesieur. *Society* My./Je. '92. **67:4**

Gambling nation. G. Hirshey. *New York Times* Jl. 17, '94. **67:4**

No limit. A. Alvarez. *New Yorker* Ag. 8, '94. **67:4**

Refuting the myths of compulsive gambling. R. E. Vatz and L. S. Weinberg. *USA Today* N.'93. **67:4**

Tricks of the trade. J. Popkin. *U.S. News & World Report* Mr. 14, '94. **67:4**
**Laws and Regulations**
Dances with sharks. D. R. Segal. *The Washington Monthly* Mr. '92. **67:4**

Gambling boom. R. L. Worsnop. *CQ Researcher* Mr. 18, '94. **67:4**

Incident at Akwesasne. D. D'Ambrosio. *Gentlemen's Quarterly* N. '93. **67:4**
**Moral and Religious Aspects**
Casino wars: ethics and economics in Indian country. J. Magnuson. *The Christian Century* F. 16, '94. **67:4**
**Psychological Aspects**
Gambler's anonymous. *Twenty Questions* '80. **67:4**

Penny ante. E. Allen. *Gentlemen's Quarterly* My. '92. **67:4**

Treatment of pathological gambling. M. C. McGurrin. *Pathological Gambling: Conceptual, Diagnostic and Treatment Issues* '94. **67:4**

Tricks of the trade. J. Popkin. *U.S. News & World Report* Mr. 14, '94. **67:4**

**GENE THERAPY**
Genetic attacks on AIDS readied. G. Kolata. *New York Times* My. 31, '94. **67:3**

Scientists develop new techniques to track down defects in genes. S. Blakeslee. *New York Times* S. 12, '89. **67:3**

The genetic revolution: designer genes. B. Merz. *American Health* Mr. '93. **67:3**

Uses and abuses of human gene transfer. W. F. Anderson. From *Human Gene Therapy* '92. **67:3**

### Genetic Mapping

Genetics: the money rush is on. G. Blinsky. *Fortune* My. 30, '94. **67:3**

### GENETIC RESEARCH

#### Environmental Aspects

The coming of the high-tech harvest. P. Weintraub. *Audubon* Jl./Ag. '92. **67:3**

#### Genetic Research Industry

A most unsatisfactory organism. S. S. Hall. From *Mapping the Next Millenium* '91. **67:3**

Genetics: the money rush is on. G. Blinsky. *Fortune* My. 30, '94. **67:3**

The organ factory of the future? D. Concar. *New Scientist* Je. 18, '94. **67:3**

#### Genetic Screening

Hunting down Huntington's. A. Revkin. *Discover* D. '93. **67:3**

To test or not to test? L. Roberts. *Science* Ja. 5, '90. **67:3**

#### Moral and Ethical Aspects

Breaking the box. G. F. Gilder. *National Review* Ag. 15, '94. **67:5**

Insurance for the insurers: the use of genetic tests. N. E. Kass. *Hastings Center Report* N./D. '92. **67:3**

Privacy rules for DNA databanks. G. J. Annas. *The Journal of the American Medical Association* N. 17, '93. **67:3**

Use of genetic testing by employers. Council on Ethical and Judicial Affairs. *Journal of the American Medical Association* O. 2, '91. **67:3**

### GOVERNMENT

#### Retirement

A farewell to public office. M. M. Cuomo. Speech delivered D. 16, '94. **67:6**

#### Republican Aims

A contract with America. N. L. Gingrich. Speech delivered Ja. 4, '95. **67:6**

### GROWTH HORMONE, SYNTHETIC

No human risks: new animal drug increases milk production. K. L. Ropp. My. '94. **67:3**

### HEMLOCK QUARTERLY

Genetic attacks on AIDS readied. G. Kolata. *New York Times* My. 31, '94. **67:3**

**HUMAN GENOME PROJECT**
### About

DNA goes to court. R. M. Cook-Deegan. From *The Gene Wars: Politics, and the Human Genome* '94. **67:3**

Taking stock of the genome project. L. Roberts. *Science* O. 1, '93. **67:3**

The human genome project. E. Edelson. *Popular Science* Jl.'91. **67:3**

**HUNTINGTON'S DISEASE**

Hunting down Huntington's. A. Revkin. *Discover* D.'93. **67:3**

**HUNTSVILLE (TEX.)**
### Prisons

Witness to another execution. S. Blaustein. *Harper's* My. '94. **67:1**

**INDIANS OF NORTH AMERICA**
### Canada

Tribal gambles: Canada's first nations jump on the gaming bandwagon. M. McDonald. *Maclean's* My. 30, '94.
### Casinos

Casino wars: ethics and economics in Indian country. J. Magnuson. *The Christian Century* F. 16, '94. **67:4**

Dances with sharks. D. R. Segal. *The Washington Monthly* Mr. '92. **67:4**

Incident at Akwesasne. D. D'Ambrosio. *Gentlemen's Quarterly* N. '93. **67:4**
### Crime

Incident at Akwesasne. D. D'Ambrosio. *Gentlemen's Quarterly* N. '93. **67:4**
### Government Relations

Dances with sharks. D. R. Segal. *The Washington Monthly* Mr. '92. **67:4**

**INFORMATION HIGHWAYS**

If this is the information superhighway, where are the rest stops? D. Baldwin. *Common Cause* Spring '94. **67:5**

Information superhighway. *The Freedom Forum* My. '94. **67:5**

Sex & the super-highway. B. Fryer. *Working Woman* Ap. '94. **67:5**

The cultural consequences of the information superhighway. T. Maddox. *Wilson Quarterly* Summer '94. **67:5**

The national information infrastructure: agenda for action. From *Executive Office of the President* '93. **67:5**

Will the information superhighway be the death of retailing? S. Sherman. *Fortune* Ap. 18, '94. **67:5**
### Laws and Regulations

A legislative agenda for telecommunications. E. J. Markey. *Issues in Science and Technology* Fall '93. **67:5**

Policymaking and policymakers. F. H. Cate. *Stanford Law & Policy Review* '94.

Who owns the law? G. Wolf. *Wired* My. '94. **67:5**

**INFORMATION SYSTEMS**
### Civilization
Breaking the box. G. F. Gilder. *National Review* Ag. 15, '94. **67:5**
### Crime
Policing cyberspace. V. Sussman. *U.S. News & World Report* Ja. 23, '95. **67:5**

Wire pirates. P. Wallich. *Scientific American* Mr.'94. **67:5**
### Philosophy
A magna carta for the knowledge age. E. Dyson, G. Gilder, J. Keyworth, and A. Toffler. *New Perspectives Quarterly* Fall '94. **67:5**
### Political Use
Democracy on-line. J. Snider. *The Futurist* S./O. '94. **67:5**

Winning votes on the information superhighway. R. S. Conrad. *Campaigns & Elections* Jl. '94. **67:5**
### Pornography
The naked city. J. Zipperer. *Christian Today* S. 12, '94. **67:5**
### Television
Breaking the box. G. F. Gilder. *National Review* Ag. 15, '94. **67:5**
### Women
Sex & the super-highway. B. Fryer. *Working Woman* Ap. '94. **67:5**

**INSURANCE, HEALTH**
### United States
Insurance for the insurers: the use of genetic tests. N. E. Kass. *Hastings Center Report* N./D. '92. **67:3**

**INSURANCE ETHICS**
Insurance for the insurers: the use of genetic tests. N. E. Kass. *Hastings Center Report* N./D.'92. **67:3**

**INTERACTIVE MARKETING**
### Internet
The history of the future. G. H. Anthes. *Computerworld* O. 3, '94. **67:5**

The underpinnings of privacy protection. F. M. Tuerkheimer. *Communications of the ACM* Ag. '93. **67:5**

Will the information superhighway be the death of retailing? S. Sherman. *Fortune* Ap. 18, '94. **67:5**
### Security Measures
Wire pirates. P. Wallich. *Science America* Mr. '94. **67:5**

**JACKSON, JESSE**
### About
Action Jackson. H. Rosin. *The New Republic* Mr. 21, '94. **67:1**

**JEWISH HISTORY**
Close your eyes, and listen to the silent screams. E. Wiesel. Speech delivered Ja. 27, '95. **67:6**

JUVENILE DELINQUENTS AND DELINQUENCY

A generation of stone killers. S. Minerbrook. *U.S. News & World Report* Ja. 17, '94. **67:1**

American killers are getting younger. J. A. Fox and G. L. Pierce. *USA Today* Ja. '94. **67:1**

**Prevention**

Violent crime: myths, facts, and solutions. D. S. Eitzen. *Vital Speeches of the Day* Speech delivered My. 15, '95. **67:6**

JUVENILE JUSTICE, ADMINISTRATION OF

When kids go bad. R. Lacayo. *Time* S. 19, '94. **67:1**

KEVORKIAN, JACK

**About**

Coming soon: your neighborhood T.S.C. P. J. Bernardi. *America* Ap. 30, '94. **67:2**

Rx for death. N. R. Gibbs. *Time* My. 31, '93. **67:2**

Death on trial. J. P. Shapiro. *U.S. News & World Report* Ap. 25, '94. **67:2**

LETHAL INJECTIONS

Witness to another execution. S. Blaustein. *Harper's* My. '94. **67:1**

MANDATORY SENTENCES

The law of unintended consequences. N. Steinberg. *Rolling Stone* My. 5, '94. **67:1**

MEDICAL POLICY

**Oregon**

The Oregon trail to death. C. S. Campbell. *Commonweal* Ag 19, '94. **67:2**

MILK PRODUCTION

New animal drug increases milk production. K. L. Ropp. *FDA Consumer* My.'94. **67:3**

MILLER, JEROME

**About**

No justice, no peace. R. Szykowny. *The Humanist* Ja./F. '94. **67:1**

MOHAWK INDIANS

Incident at Akwesasne. D. D'Ambrosio. *Gentlemen's Quarterly* N. '93. **67:4**

MURDER

American killers are getting younger. J. A. Fox and G. L. Pierce. *USA Today* Ja. '94. **67:1**

NATIONAL CENTER ON INSTITUTIONS AND ALTERNATIVES

**About**

No justice, no peace. R. Szykowny. *The Humanist* Ja./F. '94. **67:1**

OBSCENITY

The naked city. J. Zipperer. *Christian Today* S. 12, '94. **67:5**

## PARENT-CHILD RELATIONSHIP

Watching dad gamble. P. Jordan. *Yankee* Jl. '93. **67:4**

## PARENTS

Why grade "A" execs get an "F" as parents. B. O'Reilly. *Fortune* Ja. 1, '90. **67:2**

## PAROLE

A solution to prison overcrowding. J. Turley. *USA Today* N. '92. **67:1**

## PEQUOT INDIANS

Revenge of the Indians. K. I. Eisler. *The Washingtonian* Ag. '93. **67:4**

## PLANT GENETICS

Can biotech put bread on third world tables? J. E. Ellis. *Business Week* D. 14, '92. **67:3**

The coming of the high-tech harvest. P. Weintraub. *Audubon* Jl./Ag. '92. **67:3**

## POKER

No limit. A. Alvarez. *New Yorker* Ag. 8, '94. **67:4**

## PRISONERS

### Monitoring

Walking prisons. M. Winkler. *The Futurist* Jl./Ag.'93. **67:1**

### Prisons

. . . and throw away the key. J. Smolowe. *Time* F. 7, '94. **67:1**

## RIGHT TO DIE

Dead complicated. E. Rosenthal. *Discover* O.'92. **67:2**

Death with dignity. W. M. McCord. *The Humanist* Ja./F.'93. **67:2**

Last rights. K. Ames. *Newsweek* Ag. 26, '91. **67:2**

Love and let die. N. R. Gibbs. *Time* Mr. 19, '90. **67:2**

The suicide machine. N. K. Denzin. *Society* Jl./Ag. '92. **67:2**

## ROOSEVELT, FRANKLIN D.

### About

An American creed. F. F. Church IV. Speech delivered Ap. 9, '95. **67:6**

## SAINT REGIS AKWESASNE INDIAN RESERVE

Incident at Akwesasne. D. D'Ambrosio. *Gentlemen's Quarterly* N. '93. **67:4**

## STRESS

Verbal and physical abuse as stressors in the lives of lesbian, gay male, and bisexual youths. R. C. Savin-Williams. *Journal of Consulting and Clinical Psychology* Ap. '94. **67:2**

## TEENAGE SUICIDE

Jerry's choice: why are our children killing themselves? N. Wartik. *American Health* O. '91. **67:2**

**TELECOMMUNICATION**

The national information infrastructure: agenda for action. From *Executive Office of the President* '93. **67:5**

The underpinnings of privacy protection. F. M. Tuerkheimer. *Communications of the ACM* Ag. '93. **67:5**

**In Politics**

Democracy on-line. J. Snider. *The Futurist* S./O.'94. **67:5**

Electric rhetoric: the transformation of American political talk. B. E. Gronbeck. Speech delivered Mr. 24, '94. **67:6**

**Laws and Regulations**

A legislative agenda for telecommunications. E. J. Markey. *Issues in Science and Technology* Fall '93. **67:5**

If this is the information superhighway, where are the rest stops? D. Baldwin. *Common Cause* Spring '94. **67:5**

**TELEPHONE**

**Security Measures**

Wire pirates. P. Wallich. *Scientific American* Mr. '94. **67:2**

**TELEVISION BROADCASTING**

Television news reporting. A. J. Rooney. Speech delivered O. 12, '94. **67:6**

**Social Aspects**

Breaking the box. G. F. Gilder. *National Review* Ag. 15, '94. **67:5**

**UNITED STATES**

**Economic Conditions**

The digital juggernaut. M. J. Mandel. *Business Week* My. 18, '94. **67:5**

**State of the Union Address**

State of the union address. W. J. Clinton. Speech delivered Ja. 25, '94. **67:6**

**UNITED STATES. FEDERAL LAW ENFORCEMENT TRAINING CENTER**

**About**

Policing cyberspace. V. S. Sussman. *U.S. News & World Report* Ja. 23, '95. **67:5**

**UNITED STATES. SUPREME COURT**

**Decisions**

The Supreme Court and capital punishment. C. F. Murphy. *USA Today* Mr. '93. **67:1**

**VENTER, CRAIG J.**

**About**

Genetics: the money rush is on. G. Bylinsky. *Fortune* My. 30, '94. **67:3**

**VIOLENCE**

Fear and terror. F. F. Church. Speech delivered Ap. 23, '95. **67:6**

Violent crime: myths, facts, and solutions. D. S. Eitzen. *Vital Speeches of the Day* Speech delivered Mr. 15, '95. **67:6**

**WEXLER, NANCY S.**

**About**

Hunting down Huntington's. A. Revkin. *Discover* D. '93. **67:3**

**WIESEL, ELIE**

**About**

Elie Wiesel now agrees to take part in the Auschwitz rites. J. Perlez. *New York Times* Ja. 20, '95. **67:6**

**YOUTH AND FIREARMS**

American killers are getting younger. J. A. Fox and G. L. Pierce. *USA Today* Ja. '94. **67:1**